# HOME SWEET HOME Afghans

Filled with cozy wraps that reflect the loving warmth of home and family, Home Sweet Home Afghans *will be a welcome addition to your crochet library.*

*This outstanding collection includes 50 favorite throws hand-selected from Leisure Arts publications. You'll discover afghans that feature a variety of stitches and techniques for all skill levels. For quick results, choose a granny square or mile-a-minute wrap. Or, if you prefer, try one of our intricate designs at a more leisurely pace.*

*With five heartwarming sections, there are styles from fanciful to understated — each perfect for a certain room, mood, or season. In Home Fires Burn Brightest, you'll find throws ideal for cuddling by the hearth. Home for the Holidays features whimsical designs for celebrations throughout the year, and To Grandmother's House We Go offers afghans that will bring on a ripple of nostalgia. Floral motifs accent the garden-inspired wraps in Home Is Where the Heart Can Bloom, and Home Is Where the Heart Is overflows with heart-embellished cover-ups.*

*You'll feel right at home with any of the wonderful afghans in this timeless treasury!*

LEISURE ARTS, INC.
and
OXMOOR HOUSE, INC.

# EDITORIAL STAFF

**Vice President and Editor-in-Chief:** Anne Van Wagner Childs
**Executive Director:** Sandra Graham Case
**Editorial Director:** Susan Frantz Wiles
**Publications Director:** Carla Bentley
**Creative Art Director:** Gloria Bearden
**Senior Graphics Art Director:** Melinda Stout

## PRODUCTION
**Managing Editor:** Joan Gessner Beebe
**Technical Writer:** Tammy Kreimeyer

## EDITORIAL
**Managing Editor:** Linda L. Trimble
**Associate Editor:** Robyn Sheffield-Edwards
**Assistant Editors:** Tammi Williamson Bradley,
    Terri Leming Davidson, Darla Burdette Kelsay, and
    Janice Teipen Wojcik
**Copy Editor:** Laura Lee Weland

## ART
**Book/Magazine Graphics Art Director:** Diane M. Hugo
**Senior Graphics Artist:** M. Katherine Yancey
**Photography Stylists:** Christina Tiano Myers, Karen Smart Hall,
    Rhonda H. Hestir, Sondra Daniel, and Aurora Huston

# BUSINESS STAFF

**Publisher:** Bruce Akin
**Vice President, Marketing:** Guy A. Crossley
**Marketing Manager:** Byron L. Taylor
**Print Production Manager:** Laura Lockhart
**Vice President and General Manager:** Thomas L. Carlisle
**Retail Sales Director:** Richard Tignor
**Vice President, Retail Marketing:** Pam Stebbins
**Retail Marketing Director:** Margaret Sweetin
**Retail Customer Services Manager:** Carolyn Pruss
**General Merchandise Manager:** Russ Barnett
**Vice President, Finance:** Tom Siebenmorgen
**Distribution Director:** Ed M. Strackbein

**Home Sweet Home Afghans**
from the *Crochet Treasury* Series
Published by Leisure Arts, Inc., and Oxmoor House, Inc.

Library of Congress Catalog Number: 97-73648
Hardcover ISBN 0-8487-4115-3
Softcover ISBN 1-57486-053-4

# TABLE OF CONTENTS

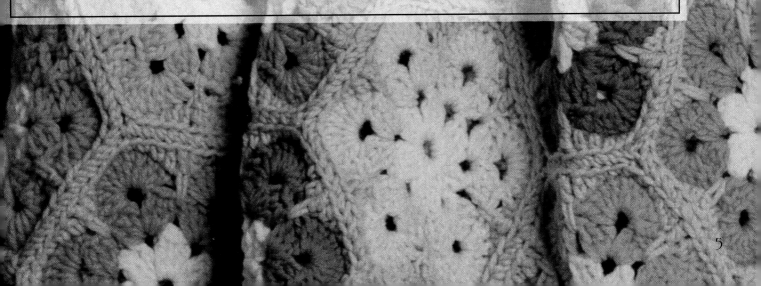

# HOME
## is where the heart can bloom

*An extension of the home and heart, the garden is a special place where endless hours are spent planting and nurturing beautiful flowers. Simply put, it's a bit of heaven here on earth! Blooming with roses, daffodils, pansies, primroses, sunflowers, and more, our collection of afghans will be admired by all who appreciate nature's artistry. These flowering inspirations are magnificent crocheted portraits of spring and summer.*

# FLORAL DAYDREAM

*A carefree afternoon in the porch swing will be extra nice when you're tucked beneath this flower-accented comforter. The springtime afghan is worked in large squares that are whipstitched together, so it's a breeze to finish!*

**Finished Size:** 50" x 66"

## MATERIALS

Worsted Weight Yarn:
- Ecru - 25 ounces, (710 grams, 1,575 yards)
- Yellow - 1/2 ounce, (20 grams, 30 yards)
- Lt Plum - 7 ounces, (200 grams, 440 yards)
- Plum - 8 ounces, (230 grams, 505 yards)
- Green - 18 ounces, (510 grams, 1,135 yards)

Crochet hook, size I (5.50 mm) **or** size needed for gauge
Yarn needle

**GAUGE:** Each Square = 15¾"

**Gauge Swatch:** 6" square
Work same as Rnds 1-10 of Square.
Finish off.

## STITCH GUIDE

> **FRONT POST HALF DOUBLE CROCHET**
> *(abbreviated FPhdc)*
> YO, insert hook from **front** to **back** around post of st indicated, YO and pull up a loop *(Fig. 11, page 122)*, YO and draw through all 3 loops on hook. Skip dc behind FPhdc.

## SQUARE (Make 12)

With Yellow, ch 4; join with slip st to form a ring.

**Rnd 1 (Right side):** Ch 1, 6 sc in ring; join with slip st to first sc.

**Note:** Loop a short piece of yarn around any stitch to mark Rnd 1 as **right** side.

**Rnd 2:** Ch 1, sc in same st, ch 2, (sc in next sc, ch 2) around; join with slip st to first sc, finish off: 6 ch-2 sps.

**Rnd 3:** With **right** side facing, join Lt Plum with slip st in any ch-2 sp; ch 1, (sc, 4 dc, sc) in same sp and in each ch-2 sp around; join with slip st to first sc: 6 petals.

**Rnd 4:** Ch 3, ★ working **behind** petal, slip st in first sc of next petal, ch 3; repeat from ★ around; join with slip st to base of beginning ch-3, finish off.

**Rnd 5:** With **right** side facing, join Plum with slip st in any ch-3 sp; ch 1, (sc, 5 dc, sc) in same sp and in each ch-3 sp around; join with slip st to first sc.

**Rnd 6:** Ch 4, ★ working **behind** petal, slip st in first sc of next petal, ch 4; repeat from ★ around; join with slip st to base of beginning ch-4, finish off.

**Rnd 7:** With **right** side facing, join Green with slip st in any ch-4 sp; ch 1, (sc, 6 dc, sc) in same sp and in each ch-4 sp around; join with slip st to first sc.

**Rnd 8:** Ch 5, ★ working **behind** petal, slip st in first sc of next petal, ch 5; repeat from ★ around; join with slip st to base of beginning ch-5, finish off.

**Rnd 9:** With **right** side facing, join Ecru with slip st in any ch-5 sp; ch 4, (2 tr, ch 3, 3 tr) in same sp, ch 1, † (3 dc, ch 1, 3 tr) in next ch-5 sp, ch 3, (3 tr, ch 1, 3 dc) in next ch-5 sp, ch 1 †, (3 tr, ch 3, 3 tr) in next ch-5 sp, ch 1, repeat from † to † once; join with slip st to top of beginning ch-4: 12 sps.

**Rnd 10:** Slip st in next 2 tr and in first ch-3 sp, ch 4, (2 tr, ch 3, 3 tr) in same sp, ch 1, (3 dc in next ch-1 sp, ch 1) twice, ★ (3 tr, ch 3, 3 tr) in next ch-3 sp, ch 1, (3 dc in next ch-1 sp, ch 1) twice; repeat from ★ around; join with slip st to top of beginning ch-4: 16 sps.

**Rnd 11:** Slip st in next 2 tr and in first ch-3 sp, ch 3 (**counts as first dc, now and throughout**), (2 dc, ch 3, 3 dc) in same sp, ch 1, (3 dc in next ch-1 sp, ch 1) 3 times, ★ (3 dc, ch 3, 3 dc) in next ch-3 sp, ch 1, (3 dc in next ch-1 sp, ch 1) 3 times; repeat from ★ around; join with slip st to first dc: 60 dc.

**Rnd 12:** Ch 3, dc in next 2 dc, 7 dc in next ch-3 sp, ★ dc in each dc and in each ch-1 sp across to next ch-3 sp, 7 dc in next ch-3 sp; repeat from ★ 2 times **more**, dc in each dc and in each ch-1 sp across; join with slip st to first dc, finish off: 104 dc.

**Rnd 13:** With **right** side facing, join Lt Plum with slip st in third dc of any 7-dc group; ch 1, sc in same st, ★ † (hdc, 3 dc, hdc) in next dc, (sc in next dc, hdc in next dc, 3 dc in next dc, hdc in next dc) 6 times †, sc in next dc; repeat from ★ 2 times **more**, then repeat from † to † once; join with slip st to first sc: 28 scallops.

**Rnd 14:** Ch 4, skip next 5 sts, working **behind** scallops, slip st in next sc, ★ (ch 3, skip next 5 sts, slip st in next sc) 6 times, ch 4, skip next 5 sts, slip st in next sc; repeat from ★ 2 times **more**, ch 3, skip next 5 sts, (slip st in next sc, ch 3, skip next 5 sts) across; join with slip st to base of beginning ch-4, finish off.

**Rnd 15:** With **right** side facing, join Green with slip st in any ch-4 sp; ch 1, (sc, hdc, 5 dc, hdc, sc) in same sp, (sc, hdc, 3 dc, hdc, sc) in each of next 6 ch-3 sps, ★ (sc, hdc, 5 dc, hdc, sc) in next ch-4 sp, (sc, hdc, 3 dc, hdc, sc) in each of next 6 ch-3 sps; repeat from ★ around; join with slip st to first sc.

**Rnd 16:** Ch 5, working **behind** scallops, slip st in first sc of next scallop, ★ (ch 3, slip st in first sc of next scallop) 6 times, ch 5, slip st in first sc of next scallop; repeat from ★ 2 times **more**, ch 3, (slip st in first sc of next scallop, ch 3) across; join with slip st to st at base of first ch, finish off.

**Rnd 17:** With **right** side facing, join Plum with slip st in any ch-5 sp; ch 1, (sc, hdc, 5 dc, hdc, sc) in same sp, (sc, hdc, 3 dc, hdc, sc) in each of next 6 ch-3 sps, ★ (sc, hdc, 5 dc, hdc, sc) in next ch-5 sp, (sc, hdc, 3 dc, hdc, sc) in each of next 6 ch-3 sps; repeat from ★ around; join with slip st to first sc.

**Rnd 18:** Ch 6, working **behind** scallops, slip st in first sc of next scallop ★ (ch 3, slip st in first sc of next scallop) 6 times, ch 6, slip st in first sc of next scallop; repeat from ★ 2 times **more**, ch 3, (slip st in first sc of next scallop) across; join with slip st to st at base of beginning ch-6, finish off.

**Rnd 19:** With **right** side facing, join Green with slip st in any ch-6 sp; ch 3, (3 dc, 3 tr, 4 dc) in same sp, 5 dc in each of next 6 ch-3 sps, ★ (4 dc, 3 tr, 4 dc) in next ch-6 sp, 5 dc in each of next 6 ch-3 sps; repeat from ★ around; join with slip st to first dc: 164 sts.

**Rnd 20:** Ch 3, dc in each st around, working 4 dc in center tr of each corner; join with slip st to first dc, finish off: 176 dc.

**Rnd 21:** With **right** side facing, join Ecru with slip st in third dc of any 4-dc group; ch 1, 3 sc in same st, ★ † work FPhdc around next dc, (sc in next dc, work FPhdc around next dc) across to third dc of next 4-dc group †, 3 sc in third dc; repeat from ★ 2 times **more**, then repeat from † to † once; join with slip st to first sc: 184 sts.

Continued on page 8.

7

**Rnd 22:** Ch 2, hdc in each st around, working 3 hdc in center sc of each corner; join with slip st to top of beginning ch-2: 192 sts.

**Rnd 23:** Ch 1, sc in same st and in each hdc around, working 3 sc in center hdc of each corner; join with slip st to first sc, finish off: 200 sc.

## ASSEMBLY

Using Ecru and working through inside loops only, whipstitch Squares together *(Fig. 26a, page 127)*, forming 3 vertical strips of 4 Squares each, beginning in center sc of first corner and ending in center sc of next corner; whipstitch strips together in same manner.

## BORDER

**Rnd 1:** With **right** side facing, join Ecru with slip st in any sc; ch 1, sc evenly around, working 3 sc in center sc of each corner; join with slip st to Back Loop Only of first sc *(Fig. 24, page 126)*.

**Rnd 2:** Ch 3; working in Back Loops Only, dc in each sc around, working 3 dc in center sc of each corner; join with slip st to Back Loop Only of first dc.

**Rnd 3:** Ch 1; working in Back Loops Only, sc in same st and in each dc around, working 3 sc in center dc of each corner; join with slip st to Back Loop Only of first sc.

**Rnd 4:** Ch 1; working in Back Loops Only, sc in same st and in each sc around, working 3 sc in center sc of each corner; join with slip st to both loops of first sc, finish off.

# PRETTY POSIES

*Resembling a patch of pretty posies, this uniquely shaped afghan features a lovely array of colors. The cheery flower motifs are super easy to create using a combination of basic stitches and long treble crochets.*

**Finished Size:** 46" x 68"

## MATERIALS

Worsted Weight Yarn:
Green - 16 ounces, (450 grams, 1,050 yards)
Yellow - 8 ounces, (230 grams, 525 yards)
Blue - 4 ounces, (110 grams, 265 yards)
Dk Blue - 4 ounces, (110 grams, 265 yards)
Pink - 4 ounces, (110 grams, 265 yards)
Dk Pink - 4 ounces, (110 grams, 265 yards)
Lavender - 4 ounces, (110 grams, 265 yards)
Dk Lavender - 4 ounces, (110 grams, 265 yards)
Peach - 4 ounces, (110 grams, 265 yards)
Dk Peach - 4 ounces, (110 grams, 265 yards)
Crochet hook, size H (5.00 mm) **or** size needed for gauge
Yarn needle

**GAUGE:** Each Motif = 4³/₄"
(straight edge to straight edge)

## STITCH GUIDE

> **LONG TREBLE CROCHET** *(abbreviated LTR)*
> YO twice, working **around** Rnd 3, insert hook in sp indicated on Rnd 2, YO and pull up a loop, (YO and draw through 2 loops on hook) 3 times *(Fig. 17, page 123)*.

**Note:** The color used on Rnds 2 and 3 of each Motif varies. Make the number of Motifs indicated with each of the following colors: Blue - 20, Dk Blue - 17, Pink - 18, Dk Pink - 19, Lavender - 19, Dk Lavender - 18, Peach - 19, and Dk Peach - 19.

## MOTIF (Make 149)

With Yellow, ch 6; join with slip st to form a ring.

**Rnd 1 (Right side):** Ch 3 **(counts as first dc, now and throughout)**, 2 dc in ring, ch 3, (3 dc in ring, ch 3) 5 times; join with slip st to first dc, finish off: 6 ch-3 sps.

**Note:** Loop a short piece of yarn around any stitch to mark Rnd 1 as **right** side.

**Rnd 2:** With **right** side facing, join next color with slip st in any ch-3 sp; ch 3, (2 dc, ch 3, 3 dc) in same sp, (3 dc, ch 3, 3 dc) in each ch-3 sp around; join with slip st to first dc: 36 dc and 6 ch-3 sps.

**Rnd 3:** Slip st in next 2 dc and in next ch-3 sp, ch 3, 8 dc in same sp, 9 dc in each ch-3 sp around; join with slip st to first dc, finish off: 54 dc.

**Rnd 4:** With **right** side facing, join Green with slip st in same st as joining; ch 2, hdc in next dc, sc in next 5 dc, hdc in next 2 dc, work LTR in sp **between** next 2 3-dc groups on Rnd 2 *(Fig. 20, page 124)*, ★ hdc in next 2 dc on Rnd 3, sc in next 5 dc, hdc in next 2 dc, work LTR in sp **between** next 2 3-dc groups on Rnd 2; repeat from ★ around; join with slip st to top of beginning ch, finish off: 60 sts.

## ASSEMBLY

Using Green, working through inside loops only, and randomly placing Motifs, whipstitch Motifs together *(Fig. 26a, page 127)*, forming 6 vertical strips of 14 Motifs each and 5 vertical strips of 13 Motifs each, beginning in third sc of first 5-sc group and ending in third sc of next 5-sc group; whipstitch strips together in same manner.

## EDGING

**Rnd 1:** With **right** side facing, join Green with sc in any st *(see Joining With Sc, page 126)*; sc evenly around, increasing and decreasing as necessary to keep piece lying flat and working an even number of sc; join with slip st to first sc.

**Rnd 2:** Ch 1, turn; sc in same st, tr in next sc, (sc in next sc, tr in next sc) around; join with slip st to first sc, finish off.

# SUNFLOWER FESTIVAL

*Give guests a cheery welcome by displaying this vibrant sunflower-touched afghan.*
*Worked in squares of deep green, the throw is completed with thick fringe.*

**Finished Size:** 48" x 62"

## MATERIALS
Worsted Weight Yarn:
Green - 33 ounces, (940 grams, 2,265 yards)
Gold - 15 ounces, (430 grams, 1,030 yards)
Brown - 11 ounces, (310 grams, 755 yards)
Crochet hook, size G (4.00 mm) **or** size needed for gauge
Yarn needle

**GAUGE:** Each Square = 6³/4"

**Gauge Swatch:** 3³/4" in diameter
Work same as Square through Rnd 2.

## STITCH GUIDE

BEGINNING 2-TR CLUSTER
Ch 3, tr in same st.
2-TR CLUSTER
★ YO twice, insert hook in st indicated, YO and pull up a loop, (YO and draw through 2 loops on hook) twice; repeat from ★ once **more**, YO and draw through all 3 loops on hook *(Figs. 16a & b, page 123)*.
BEGINNING 5-TR CLUSTER
Ch 3, ★ YO twice, insert hook in **same** sp, YO and pull up a loop, (YO and draw through 2 loops on hook) twice; repeat from ★ 3 times **more**, YO and draw through all 5 loops on hook.
5-TR CLUSTER
★ YO twice, insert hook in sp indicated, YO and pull up a loop, (YO and draw through 2 loops on hook) twice; repeat from ★ 4 times **more**, YO and draw through all 6 loops on hook.
DECREASE
† YO twice, insert hook in **next** sp, YO and pull up a loop, (YO and draw through 2 loops on hook) twice †, YO twice, insert hook in joining, YO and pull up a loop, (YO and draw through 2 loops on hook) twice, repeat from † to † once, YO and draw through all 4 loops on hook.

## SQUARE (Make 63)
With Brown, ch 5; join with slip st to form a ring.
**Rnd 1 (Right side):** Ch 3, 15 dc in ring; join with slip st to top of beginning ch-3: 16 sts.

**Note:** Loop a short piece of yarn around any stitch to mark Rnd 1 as **right** side.
**Rnd 2:** Work beginning 2-tr Cluster, ch 2, (work 2-tr Cluster in next dc, ch 2) around; join with slip st to top of beginning 2-tr Cluster, finish off: 16 2-tr Clusters.
**Rnd 3:** With **right** side facing, join Gold with slip st in any ch-2 sp; work beginning 5-tr Cluster, ch 3, (work 5-tr Cluster in next ch-2 sp, ch 3) around; join with slip st to top of beginning 5-tr Cluster, finish off: 16 5-tr Clusters.
**Rnd 4:** With **right** side facing, join Green with slip st in any ch-3 sp; ch 4 **(counts as first tr)**, 3 tr in same sp, 4 dc in next ch-3 sp, 4 hdc in next ch-3 sp, 4 dc in next ch-3 sp, ★ (4 tr, ch 1, 4 tr) in next ch-3 sp, 4 dc in next ch-3 sp, 4 hdc in next ch-3 sp, 4 dc in next ch-3 sp; repeat from ★ 2 times **more**, 4 tr in same sp as first tr, sc in first tr to form last ch-1 sp: 80 sts and 4 ch-1 sps.
**Rnd 5:** Ch 3, (dc, ch 2, 2 dc) in same sp, dc in next tr and in each st across to next corner ch-1 sp, ★ (2 dc, ch 2, 2 dc) in corner ch-1 sp, dc in each st across to next corner ch-1 sp; repeat from ★ 2 times **more**; join with slip st to top of beginning ch-3, finish off: 96 sts and 4 ch-2 sps.

## ASSEMBLY
Using Green and working through both loops, whipstitch Squares together *(Fig. 26b, page 127)*, forming 7 vertical strips of 9 Squares each, beginning in second ch of first corner ch-2 and ending in first ch of next corner ch-2; whipstitch strips together in same manner.

## EDGING
With **right** side facing, join Green with slip st in any corner ch-2 sp; ch 3, (dc, ch 1, 2 dc) in same sp, dc in next 24 sts, (decrease, dc in next 24 sts) across to next corner ch-2 sp, ★ (2 dc, ch 1, 2 dc) in corner ch-2 sp, dc in next 24 sts, (decrease, dc in next 24 sts) across to next corner ch-2 sp; repeat from ★ 2 times **more**; join with slip st to top of beginning ch-3, finish off.

Holding 4 strands of Green together, add fringe evenly across short edges of Afghan *(Figs. 28a & c, page 127)*.

# COUNTRY GARDEN

*Inspired by the beloved blooms of yesteryear, this afghan features lavish flowers formed with puff stitches. These country blossoms are ideal for using up scrap yarn.*

**Finished Size:** 52" x 65"

## MATERIALS

Worsted Weight Yarn:
- Black - 38 ounces, (1,080 grams, 2,605 yards)
- Green - 10 ounces, (280 grams, 685 yards)
- Yellow - 3 ounces, (90 grams, 205 yards)
- Lt Peach -1 ounce, (30 grams, 70 yards)
- Peach - 1 ounce, (30 grams, 70 yards)
- Rust - 1 ounce, (30 grams, 70 yards)
- Lt Rose - 1 ounce, (30 grams, 70 yards)
- Rose - 1 ounce, (30 grams, 70 yards)
- Dk Rose - 1 ounce, (30 grams, 70 yards)
- Lt Purple - 1 ounce, (30 grams, 70 yards)
- Purple - 1 ounce, (30 grams, 70 yards)
- Dk Purple - 1 ounce, (30 grams, 70 yards)

Crochet hook, size I (5.50 mm) **or** size needed for gauge
Yarn needle

**GAUGE:** Each Square = 4¹/2"
Each Strip = 6¹/2" wide

## STITCH GUIDE

> **PUFF ST**
> ★ YO, insert hook around post of st indicated **(Fig. 10, page 122)**, YO and pull up a loop even with loop on hook; repeat from ★ 3 times **more**, YO and draw through all 9 loops on hook **(Fig. 15, page 122)**.
>
> **BEGINNING CLUSTER**
> Ch 2, ★ YO, insert hook in st indicated, YO and pull up a loop, YO and draw through 2 loops on hook; repeat from ★ once **more**, YO and draw through all 3 loops on hook **(Figs. 16a & b, page 123)**.
>
> **CLUSTER**
> ★ YO, insert hook in st indicated, YO and pull up a loop, YO and draw through 2 loops on hook; repeat from ★ 2 times **more**, YO and draw through all 4 loops on hook.

*Note:* The color used on Rnd 2 of each Square varies. Make a total of 112 Squares with the following colors: Lt Peach, Peach, Rust, Lt Rose, Rose, Dk Rose, Lt Purple, Purple, and Dk Purple.

## SQUARE (Make 112)

With Yellow, ch 4; join with slip st to form a ring.

**Rnd 1 (Right side):** Ch 5 **(counts as first dc plus ch 2, now and throughout)**, (dc in ring, ch 2) 5 times; join with slip st to first dc, finish off: 6 ch-2 sps.

*Note:* Loop a short piece of yarn around any stitch to mark Rnd 1 as **right** side.

**Rnd 2:** With **right** side facing, join yarn with slip st around post of any dc on Rnd 1; ch 3, work Puff St around same st, ch 5, (work Puff St around next dc, ch 5) around; join with slip st to top of first Puff St, finish off: 6 ch-5 sps.

**Rnd 3:** With **right** side facing, join Green with slip st in any ch-5 sp; ch 3 **(counts as first dc, now and throughout)**, (2 dc, ch 2, 3 dc) in same sp, (3 dc, ch 2, 3 dc) in each ch-5 sp around; join with slip st to first dc, finish off: 36 dc and 6 ch-2 sps.

**Rnd 4:** With **right** side facing, join Black with slip st in any ch-2 sp; ch 1, sc in same sp, † dc in next dc, 2 tr in next dc, tr in next dc, 2 dc in next dc, hdc in next dc, sc in next dc, 2 sc in next ch-2 sp, place marker around last sc made, sc in next dc, hdc in next dc, 2 dc in next dc, tr in next dc, 2 tr in next dc, dc in next dc, sc in next ch-2 sp and in next 6 dc †, sc in next ch-2 sp, repeat from † to † once; join with slip st to first sc: 52 sts.

**Rnd 5:** Ch 1, sc in same st and in next 2 sts, 3 sc in next tr, ★ sc in next 12 sts, 3 sc in next tr; repeat from ★ 2 times **more**, sc in last 9 sts; join with slip st to first sc, finish off: 60 sc.

## STRIP (Make 8)

### STRIP ASSEMBLY

Using Black, placing marked edges together, and working through inside loops only, whipstitch 14 randomly placed Squares together **(Fig. 26a, page 127)**, beginning in center sc of first corner 3-sc group and ending in center sc of next corner 3-sc group. Do **not** join Strips.

### STRIP BORDER

**Rnd 1:** With **right** side facing and working across short end, join Black with slip st in center sc of corner 3-sc group at top right of Strip; ch 1, 3 sc in same st, † sc in next 7 sc, skip next sc, sc in next 6 sc, 3 sc in next sc, work 197 sc evenly spaced across to center sc of next corner 3-sc group †, 3 sc in center sc, repeat from † to † once; join with slip st to first sc: 432 sc.

**Rnd 2:** Slip st in next sc, work (beginning Cluster, ch 2, Cluster) in same st, ★ ch 2, skip next sc, sc in next sc, ch 2, skip next sc, (work Cluster in next sc, ch 2, skip next sc, sc in next sc, ch 2, skip next sc) across to center sc of next corner, work (Cluster, ch 2, Cluster) in center sc; repeat from ★ 2 times **more**, ch 2, skip next sc, sc in next sc, ch 2, skip next sc, (work Cluster in next sc, ch 2, skip next sc, sc in next sc, ch 2, skip next sc) across; join with slip st to top of beginning Cluster: 112 Clusters.

**Rnd 3:** Ch 1, sc in same st, 3 sc in corner ch-2 sp, sc in next Cluster, ★ (2 sc in each of next 2 ch-2 sps, sc in next Cluster) across to next corner ch-2 sp, 3 sc in corner ch-2 sp, sc in next Cluster; repeat from ★ 2 times **more**, (2 sc in each of next 2 ch-2 sps, sc in next Cluster) across; join with slip st to first sc, finish off: 556 sc.

## ASSEMBLY

With Black, whipstitch Strips together in same manner.

# PANSY ROMANCE

*Beautiful crocheted pansies border this feminine afghan. The lacy wrap will make an endearing gift for the romantic-at-heart who recalls that Victorians sent the flowers to say "you are in my thoughts."*

**Finished Size:** 46" x 66"

## MATERIALS
Worsted Weight Yarn:
Ecru - 32 ounces, (910 grams, 2,195 yards)
Black - 2 ounces, (60 grams, 135 yards)
Gold - 1 ounce, (30 grams, 70 yards)
Yellow - 3/4 ounce, (20 grams, 50 yards)
Lt Purple - 3/4 ounce, (20 grams, 50 yards)
Purple - 3/4 ounce, (20 grams, 50 yards)
Dk Purple - 3/4 ounce, (20 grams, 50 yards)
Lt Blue - 3/4 ounce, (20 grams, 50 yards)
Blue - 3/4 ounce, (20 grams, 50 yards)
Dk Blue - 3/4 ounce, (20 grams, 50 yards)
Lt Rose - 3/4 ounce, (20 grams, 50 yards)
Rose - 3/4 ounce, (20 grams, 50 yards)
Crochet hook, size H (5.00 mm) **or** size needed for gauge

**GAUGE:** In pattern, 2 repeats and 8 rows = 4"
Each Pansy = 3" wide
(small Petal to small Petal)

## STITCH GUIDE

> **LONG SC (abbreviated LSC)**
> Insert hook from front to back **around** center ring of Pansy **between** second and third 3-dc groups, YO and pull up a loop, YO and draw through both loops on hook *(Fig. 18, page 123)*.
> **PICOT**
> Ch 4, sc in third ch from hook.

## PANSY (Make 40)
Using the following colors for Rnds 2-4, make 4 Pansies with each of the following colors: Gold, Yellow, Lt Purple, Purple, Dk Purple, Lt Blue, Blue, Dk Blue, Lt Rose, and Rose.

With Black, ch 4; join with slip st to form a ring.
**Rnd 1** (Right side): Ch 3 **(counts as first dc, now and throughout)**, 2 dc in ring, (ch 3, 3 dc in ring) 3 times changing to Gold in last dc *(Fig. 23a, page 126)*, ch 5, work LSC, ch 5; join with slip st to first dc, finish off: 3 ch-3 sps and 2 ch-5 sps.
*Note:* Loop a short piece of yarn around any stitch to mark Rnd 1 as **right** side.

**Rnd 2:** With **right** side facing, join next color with slip st in second ch-5 sp to right of joining; ch 1, in same sp work [sc, ch 3, hdc, ch 1, (dc, ch 1) 5 times, hdc, ch 3, sc] **(large Petal made)**, sc in next LSC, work large Petal in next ch-5 sp, skip next dc, sc in next dc, ★ (3 dc, ch 1, 3 dc) in next ch-3 sp **(small Petal made)**, skip next dc, sc in next dc; repeat from ★ 2 times **more**; join with slip st to first sc.
**Rnd 3:** Ch 3, (sc in next sp, ch 3) 8 times, skip next sc, sc in next sc, ch 3, (sc in next sp, ch 3) 8 times, skip next sc, slip st in next sc, leave 3 small Petals unworked.
**Rnd 4:** Ch 4, working **behind** Petals, (sc in next sc **between** Petals, ch 4) 3 times, (slip st in center dc on Rnd 2 of next large Petal, ch 4) twice, place marker around last ch-4 made for joining placement; join with slip st to next slip st on Rnd 3, finish off: 6 ch-4 sps.

## CENTER
With Ecru, ch 127 **loosely**.
**Row 1** (Right side): Sc in second ch from hook, skip next 2 chs, dc in next ch, (ch 1, dc in same ch) twice, skip next 2 chs, sc in next ch, ★ ch 3, sc in next ch, skip next 2 chs, dc in next ch, (ch 1, dc in same ch) twice, skip next 2 chs, sc in next ch; repeat from ★ across: 54 dc and 17 ch-3 sps.
*Note:* Mark Row 1 as **right** side.
**Row 2:** Ch 7 **(counts as first tr plus ch 3, now and throughout)**, turn; skip next dc, (sc, ch 3) twice in next dc, ★ dc in next ch-3 sp, ch 3, skip next dc, (sc, ch 3) twice in next dc; repeat from ★ across to last sc, tr in last sc: 54 ch-3 sps.
**Row 3:** Ch 1, turn; sc in first tr, skip next ch-3 sp, dc in next ch-3 sp, (ch 1, dc in same sp) twice, ★ (sc, ch 3, sc) in next dc, skip next ch-3 sp, dc in next ch-3 sp, (ch 1, dc in same sp) twice; repeat from ★ across to last tr, sc in last tr: 54 dc and 17 ch-3 sps.
Repeat Rows 2 and 3 until Afghan measures 56" from beginning ch, ending by working Row 3; do **not** finish off.

Continued on page 16.

## EDGING

**Rnd 1:** Ch 1, do **not** turn; sc in last sc on last row, place marker around sc just made to mark corner; work 223 sc evenly spaced across end of rows; working in free loops of beginning ch (*Fig. 25b, page 126*), sc in first ch, place marker around sc just made to mark corner, work 144 sc evenly spaced across, place marker around last sc made to mark corner; work 223 sc evenly spaced across end of rows; working in sts across last row, sc in first sc, place marker around sc just made to mark corner, work 143 sc evenly spaced across; join with slip st to first sc: 736 sc.

**Rnd 2:** Ch 8 (**counts as first dc plus ch 5**), dc in same st, ch 3, skip next 3 sc, (dc in next sc, ch 3, skip next 3 sc) across to next corner sc, ★ (dc, ch 5, dc) in corner sc, ch 3, skip next 3 sc, (dc in next sc, ch 3, skip next 3 sc) across to next corner sc; repeat from ★ 2 times **more**; join with slip st to first dc: 184 ch-3 sps and 4 ch-5 sps.

*Note:* When working Rnd 3, choose Pansy color randomly.

**Rnd 3** (Joining rnd): Slip st in first corner ch-5 sp, ch 1, sc in same sp, ch 3, with **wrong** sides of **first** Pansy and Center together, sc in marked ch-4 sp on **Pansy** (*Fig. 21, page 124*), ch 3, sc in same sp on **Center**, (ch 3, sc in next ch-4 sp on **Pansy**, ch 3, sc in **same** sp on **Center**) twice, ★ † (work Picot, ch 1, sc in next ch-3 sp) twice, ch 3, with **wrong** sides of **next** Pansy and Center together, sc in marked ch-4 sp on **Pansy**, ch 3, sc in next ch-3 sp on **Center**, (ch 3, sc in next ch-4 sp on **Pansy**, ch 3, sc in next ch-3 sp on **Center**) twice †, repeat from † to † across to within one ch-3 sp of next corner ch-5 sp, work Picot, ch 1, sc in next ch-3 sp, work Picot, ch 1, sc in corner ch-5 sp, with **wrong** sides of **next** Pansy and Center together, sc in marked ch-4 sp on **Pansy**, ch 3, sc in same sp on **Center**, (ch 3, sc in next ch-4 sp on **Pansy**, ch 3, sc in **same** sp on **Center**) twice; repeat from ★ 2 times **more**, then repeat from † to † across to last ch-3 sp, work Picot, ch 1, sc in last ch-3 sp, work Picot, ch 1; join with slip st to first sc, finish off.

**Rnd 4:** With **right** side facing, join Ecru with slip st in first sc to right of joining; ch 3, working around **first** Pansy, (tr, ch 2) 3 times in first ch-4 sp (same sp as joining sc) and in each of next 3 ch-4 sps, tr in next ch-4 sp (same sp as joining sc), (ch 2, tr in same sp) twice, skip next Picot on Center, dc in next sc, ★ † working around **next** Pansy, (tr, ch 3) twice in first ch-4 sp (same sp as joining sc) and in each of next 3 ch-4 sps, (tr, ch 3, tr) in next ch-4 sp (same sp as joining sc), skip next Picot on Center, dc in next sc †, repeat from † to † across to next corner Pansy, working around corner Pansy, (tr, ch 2) 3 times in first ch-4 sp (same sp as joining sc) and in each of next 3 ch-4 sps, tr in next ch-4 sp (same sp as joining sc), (ch 2, tr in same sp) twice, skip next Picot on Center, dc in next sc; repeat from ★ 2 times **more**, then repeat from † to † across to last Pansy, working around **last** Pansy, (tr, ch 3) twice in first ch-4 sp (same sp as joining sc) and in each of next 3 ch-4 sps, (tr, ch 3, tr) in next ch-4 sp (same sp as joining sc); join with slip st to first dc.

**Rnd 5:** Slip st in next tr and in first ch-2 sp, ch 1, sc in same sp, (work Picot, ch 1, sc in next ch-2 sp) 13 times, [sc in next ch-3 sp, (work Picot, ch 1, sc in next ch-3 sp) 8 times] across to next corner Pansy, ★ sc in next ch-2 sp, (work Picot, ch 1, sc in next ch-2 sp) 13 times, [sc in next ch-3 sp, (work Picot, ch 1, sc in next ch-3 sp) 8 times] across to next corner Pansy; repeat from ★ 2 times **more**; join with slip st to first sc, finish off.

# PRIMROSE PATH

*Rows of cluster stitches form a path of dainty primroses on this quick mile-a-minute afghan. The enchanting flower is an English garden favorite.*

**Finished Size:** 45" x 64"

## MATERIALS
Worsted Weight Yarn:
 Lavender - 17 ounces, (480 grams, 1,075 yards)
 Ecru - 15 ounces, (430 grams, 950 yards)
 Green - 9 ounces, (260 grams, 570 yards)
Crochet hook, size K (6.50 mm) **or** size needed for gauge

**GAUGE:** 13 sc = 5"
 Each Strip = 4½" wide

## STITCH GUIDE

**CLUSTER**
★ YO, insert hook in st or sp indicated, YO and pull up a loop, YO and draw through 2 loops on hook; repeat from ★ once **more**, YO and draw through all 3 loops on hook (*Figs. 16a & b, page 123*).

## FIRST STRIP

With Lavender, ch 153 **loosely**.

**Foundation Row** (Right side): Sc in back ridge of second ch from hook and each ch across (*Fig. 2c, page 120*): 152 sc.

*Note:* Loop a short piece of yarn around any stitch to mark Foundation Row as **right** side.

**Rnd 1:** Slip st in end of Foundation Row, ch 2, dc in same row **(beginning Cluster made)**, (ch 3, work Cluster) twice in same row; working in free loops of beginning ch **(Fig. 25b, page 126)**, † skip first 2 sts, ★ work (Cluster, ch 3, Cluster) in next st, skip next 2 sts; repeat from ★ 49 times **more** †; work Cluster in end of Foundation Row, (ch 3, work Cluster) twice in same row; working across sc on Foundation Row, repeat from † to † once; join with slip st to top of beginning Cluster, finish off: 104 ch-3 sps.

**Rnd 2:** With **right** side facing, join Ecru with slip st in first ch-3 sp to left of joining; ch 1, (2 sc, ch 1) twice in same sp and in each ch-3 sp around; join with slip st to first sc, finish off: 208 ch-1 sps.

**Rnd 3:** With **right** side facing, join Green with slip st in second ch-1 sp to right of joining; ch 1, sc in same sp, † ch 2, work Cluster in next ch-1 sp, ch 2, sc in next ch-1 sp, ch 2, work (Cluster, ch 3, Cluster) in next ch-1 sp, ch 2, sc in next ch-1 sp, ch 2, work Cluster in next ch-1 sp, ch 2, ★ sc in next ch-1 sp, ch 1, work Cluster in next ch-1 sp, ch 1; repeat from ★ 48 times **more** †, sc in next ch-1 sp, repeat from † to † once; join with slip st to first sc, finish off: 210 sps.

**Rnd 4:** With **right** side facing, join Ecru with slip st in second ch-2 sp to left of joining; ch 2, (dc, ch 2, work Cluster) in same sp, ch 2, † [sc in next ch-2 sp, ch 2, (work Cluster, ch 2) twice in next sp] 2 times, sc in next 2 sps, (ch 4, sc in next 2 sps) 49 times, ch 2 †, (work Cluster, ch 2) twice in next ch-2 sp, repeat from † to † once; join with slip st to top of beginning Cluster, finish off: 116 sps.

# REMAINING 9 STRIPS

Work same as First Strip through Rnd 3: 210 sps.

**Rnd 4** (Joining rnd)**:** With **right** side facing, join Ecru with slip st in second ch-2 sp to left of joining; ch 2, (dc, ch 2, work Cluster) in same sp, ch 2, [sc in next ch-2 sp, ch 2, (work Cluster, ch 2) twice in next sp] 2 times, sc in next 2 sps, (ch 4, sc in next 2 sps) 49 times, ch 2, (work Cluster, ch 2) twice in next ch-2 sp, [sc in next ch-2 sp, ch 2, (work Cluster, ch 2) twice in next sp] 2 times, sc in next 2 sps, ch 2, holding Strips with **wrong** sides together, ★ slip st in corresponding ch-4 sp on **previous** Strip **(Fig. 21, page 124)**, ch 2, sc in next 2 sps on **new** Strip, ch 2; repeat from ★ across; join with slip st to top of beginning Cluster, finish off.

# WILDFLOWER BOUQUETS

*A sweet reminder of the simple wildflower bouquets we presented
to Mom as children, this floral afghan is a sentimental choice!
An edging of perfect points finishes the delicate wrap.*

**Finished Size:** 47" x 64"

## MATERIALS
Worsted Weight Yarn:
    Ecru - 32 ounces, (910 grams, 2,195 yards)
    Yellow - 2 ounces, (60 grams, 135 yards)
    Purple - 4 ounces, (110 grams, 275 yards)
    Pink - 4 ounces, (110 grams, 275 yards)
    Blue - 4 ounces, (110 grams, 275 yards)
    Green - 2 ounces, (60 grams, 135 yards)
Crochet hook, size I (5.50 mm) **or** size needed for gauge
Yarn needle

**GAUGE:** Each Square = 8¹/₂"

Gauge Swatch: 3" from tip to tip
Work same as Square Flower.

## STITCH GUIDE

> **PICOT**
> Ch 1, sc in top of tr just made.
> **POINT**
> Ch 5 **loosely**, slip st in second ch from hook, hdc in next
> ch, dc in next ch, tr in last ch.

## SQUARE (Make 35)
*Note:* The color used on Rnd 2 of each Flower varies. Make
one Flower with each of the following Petal colors: Purple,
Pink, and Blue.

### FLOWER (Make 3)
**Rnd 1 (Right side):** With Yellow and leaving a long end for
sewing, ch 3, 8 hdc in third ch from hook; join with slip st
to first hdc, finish off: 8 hdc.
*Note:* Loop a short piece of yarn around any stitch to mark
Rnd 1 as **right** side.
**Rnd 2 (Petals):** With **right** side facing, join next color with
slip st in any hdc; ch 4 **(counts as first tr)**, (tr in same hdc,
work Picot) twice, ch 4, ★ slip st in same st and in next
hdc, ch 4, (tr in same st, work Picot) twice, ch 4; repeat
from ★ 6 times **more**, slip st in same st; finish off: 8 Petals.
Thread yarn needle with beginning end and weave through
base of Rnd 1; pull **tightly** to close and secure end.

## LEAVES
**First Leaf:** With Green, ch 9 **loosely**, working in back
ridges of chs **(Fig. 2c, page 120)**, slip st in second ch from
hook, hdc in next ch, dc in next 5 chs, hdc in last ch;
do **not** finish off.
**Second Leaf:** Ch 11 **loosely**, working in back ridges of chs,
slip st in second ch from hook, hdc in next ch, dc in next
7 chs, hdc in last ch; do **not** finish off.
**Last Leaf:** Ch 9 **loosely**, working in back ridges of chs,
slip st in second ch from hook, hdc in next ch, dc in next
5 chs, hdc in last ch, slip st in last hdc on First Leaf;
finish off leaving a long end for sewing.

## BORDER
**Rnd 1:** With **right** side facing and working in Petals on
Purple Flower, skip first 2 tr on any Petal and join Ecru with
sc in next tr **(see Joining With Sc, page 126)**; † ch 3, skip
first 2 tr on next Petal, dc in next tr, ch 5, skip first 2 tr on
next Petal, dc in next tr, ch 3, skip first 2 tr on next Petal,
sc in next tr †, ch 3; with **right** side of Pink Flower facing,
skip first 2 tr on any Petal, sc in next tr, repeat from † to †
once, ch 3; with **right** side of Blue Flower facing, skip first
2 tr on any Petal, sc in next tr, repeat from † to † once, ch 4;
with **right** side of Leaves facing, sc in end of First Leaf, ch 2;
working in free loops of beginning ch on Second Leaf
**(Fig. 25b, page 126)**, skip first 7 chs, dc in next ch, ch 5,
skip first slip st and next hdc on same Leaf, dc in next dc,
ch 2, sc in end of Last Leaf, ch 4; join with slip st to first sc:
16 sts and 16 sps.
**Rnd 2:** Ch 3 **(counts as first dc, now and throughout)**,
3 dc in next ch-3 sp, dc in next dc, (3 dc, ch 3, 3 dc) in
next ch-5 sp, dc in next dc, ★ (3 dc in next sp, dc in next
st) 3 times, (3 dc, ch 3, 3 dc) in next ch-5 sp, dc in next dc;
repeat from ★ 2 times **more**, 2 dc in next ch-2 sp, dc in
next sc, 4 dc in last ch-4 sp; join with slip st to first dc:
76 dc.
**Rnd 3:** Ch 3, dc in next dc and in each dc across to next
ch-3 sp, (2 dc, ch 2, 2 dc) in ch-3 sp, ★ dc in each dc across
to next ch-3 sp, (2 dc, ch 2, 2 dc) in ch-3 sp; repeat from ★
2 times **more**, dc in each dc across; join with slip st to first
dc: 92 dc.
**Rnd 4:** Ch 3, dc in next dc and in each dc across to next
ch-2 sp, (2 dc, ch 2, 2 dc) in ch-2 sp, ★ dc in each dc across
to next ch-2 sp, (2 dc, ch 2, 2 dc) in ch-2 sp; repeat from ★
2 times **more**, dc in each dc across; join with slip st to first
dc: 108 dc.

**Rnd 5:** Ch 1, sc in same st, ★ sc in each dc across to next ch-2 sp, 3 sc in ch-2 sp; repeat from ★ 3 times **more**, sc in each dc across; join with slip st to first dc, finish off: 120 sc. Using photo as a guide for placement, overlap Flowers and Leaves and pin in place. Measure across Square and adjust placement of Flowers and Leaves as needed to maintain an 8¹/₂" square. Thread yarn needle with yarn end on Last Leaf and stitch Flowers and Leaves securely in place on wrong side.

## ASSEMBLY
Using photo as a guide, join Squares together, positioning Leaves randomly, to form 5 vertical strips of 7 Squares each. Join Squares as follows:

With **right** sides together and working through outside loops of **each** sc on **both** pieces, join Ecru with sc in center sc of first corner 3-sc group; sc in each sc across to center sc of next corner 3-sc group, sc in center sc; finish off.

Continued on page 20.

Join Strips as follows:

With **right** sides together and working through outside loops of **each** sc on **both** pieces, join Ecru with sc in center sc of first corner 3-sc group; sc in each sc across to center sc of next corner 3-sc group on same Square, ★ ch 1, skip center sc, sc in joining, ch 1, skip center sc of corner 3-sc group on next Square, sc in each sc across to next corner 3-sc group on same Square; repeat from ★ across, sc in center sc; finish off.

# EDGING

**Rnd 1:** With **right** side facing and working in Back Loops Only *(Fig. 24, page 126)*, join Ecru with sc in center sc of any corner 3-sc group; sc in same st and in next 29 sc, † sc in same st as joining on same Square, hdc in next joining, sc in same st as joining on next Square and in next 29 sc †, repeat from † to † across to center sc of next corner 3-sc group, ★ 3 sc in center sc, sc in next 29 sc, repeat from † to † across to center sc of next corner 3-sc group; repeat from ★ 2 times **more**, sc in same st as first sc; join with slip st to **both** loops of first sc, finish off: 768 sts.

**Rnd 2:** With **right** side facing and working in both loops, join Blue with slip st in same st as joining; ch 2 (**counts as first hdc**), 2 hdc in same st, ★ hdc in each sc across to center sc of next corner 3-sc group, 3 hdc in center sc; repeat from ★ 2 times **more**, hdc in each sc across; join with slip st to first hdc, finish off: 776 hdc.

**Rnd 3:** With **right** side facing, join Ecru with sc in same st as joining; sc in each hdc around; join with slip st to first sc.

**Rnd 4:** Work Point, skip next 3 sc, ★ slip st in next sc, work Point, skip next 3 sc; repeat from ★ around; join with slip st to st at base of first Point: 194 Points.

**Rnd 5:** ★ Working in free loops of ch on Point, slip st **loosely** in next 4 chs and in top of Point, slip st **loosely** in next 4 sts; repeat from ★ around; join with slip st to first slip st, finish off.

# DOGWOOD BLOSSOMS

*Bring a touch of spring indoors with this cozy afghan showcasing dogwood blossoms. Cluster stitches give the flowers texture.*

**Finished Size:** 51" x 69"

## MATERIALS

Worsted Weight Yarn:
Rose - 20 ounces, (570 grams, 900 yards)
Green - 21 ounces, (600 grams, 945 yards)
Ecru - 41 ounces, (1,160 grams, 1,845 yards)
Crochet hook, size I (5.50 mm) **or** size needed for gauge
Yarn needle

**GAUGE:** Each Square = 6¼"

## STITCH GUIDE

**BEGINNING CLUSTER** (uses next 5 tr)
Ch 3, ★ YO twice, insert hook in **next** tr, YO and pull up a loop, (YO and draw through 2 loops on hook) twice; repeat from ★ 4 times **more**, YO and draw through all 6 loops on hook *(Figs. 16c & d page 123)*.
**CLUSTER** (uses next 6 tr)
★ YO twice, insert hook in **next** tr, YO and pull up a loop, (YO and draw through 2 loops on hook) twice; repeat from ★ 5 times **more**, YO and draw through all 7 loops on hook.

## SQUARE (Make 88)

With Rose, ch 8; join with slip st to form a ring.

**Rnd 1 (Right side):** Ch 4 (**counts as first tr, now and throughout**), 5 tr in ring, ch 3, (6 tr in ring, ch 3) 3 times; join with slip st to first tr: 24 tr and 4 ch-3 sps.

*Note:* Loop a short piece of yarn around any stitch to mark Rnd 1 as **right** side.

**Rnd 2:** Work beginning Cluster, ch 5, skip next ch, slip st in next ch, ch 5, ★ work Cluster, ch 5, skip next ch, slip st in next ch, ch 5; repeat from ★ around; join with slip st to top of beginning Cluster, finish off: 4 Clusters.

**Rnd 3:** With **right** side facing, join Green with slip st in any Cluster; working **around** next slip st, (3 tr, ch 1, 3 tr, ch 2, 3 tr, ch 1, 3 tr) in next ch-3 sp on Rnd 1, ★ slip st in next Cluster, working **around** next slip st, (3 tr, ch 1, 3 tr, ch 2, 3 tr, ch 1, 3 tr) in next ch-3 sp on Rnd 1; repeat from ★ around; join with slip st to first slip st, finish off: 48 tr.

**Rnd 4:** With **right** side facing, join Ecru with slip st in any ch-2 sp; ch 4, (5 tr, ch 2, 6 tr) in same sp, 6 tr in next slip st, ★ (6 tr, ch 2, 6 tr) in next ch-2 sp, 6 tr in next slip st; repeat from ★ around; join with slip st to first tr: 72 tr.

**Rnd 5:** Ch 5, skip next 2 tr, sc in next 3 tr, ch 1, (dc, ch 1) 3 times in next ch-2 sp, skip next tr, sc in next 3 tr, ch 2, skip next 2 tr, dc in next tr, ch 2, skip next 2 tr, sc in next tr, ch 2,

skip next 2 tr, ★ dc in next tr, ch 2, skip next 2 tr, sc in next 3 tr, ch 1, (dc, ch 1) 3 times in next ch-2 sp, skip next tr, sc in next 3 tr, ch 2, skip next 2 tr, dc in next tr, ch 2, skip next 2 tr, sc in next tr, ch 2, skip next 2 tr; repeat from ★ around; join with slip st to third ch of beginning ch-5, finish off: 48 sts and 32 sps.

## ASSEMBLY

Using Ecru and working through both loops, whipstitch Squares together (*Fig. 26b, page 127*), forming 8 vertical strips of 11 Squares each, beginning in center dc of first corner and ending in center dc of next corner; whipstitch strips together in same manner.

## EDGING

With **right** side facing, join Ecru with slip st in center dc of any corner; ch 1, 3 sc in same st, sc evenly around working 3 sc in center dc of each corner; join with slip st to first sc, finish off.

21

# ROSY LULLABY

*Your little one will drift off to a happy dreamland snuggled beneath this tranquil wrap. Adorned with pink roses and a ribbon-embellished ruffle, the luxurious baby afghan is sure to become a keepsake.*

**Finished Size:** 36" x 45"

## MATERIALS
Sport Weight Yarn:
- White - 10 ounces, (280 grams, 1,065 yards)
- Pink - 8$^1$/$_2$ ounces, (240 grams, 905 yards)
- Green - 3$^1$/$_2$ ounces, (100 grams, 370 yards)

Crochet hook, size G (4.00 mm) **or** size needed for gauge
Yarn needle
5$^1$/$_2$ yards of $^3$/$_8$"w ribbon

**GAUGE:** Rnds 1-8 = 3"
Each Square = 4$^1$/$_2$"

## STITCH GUIDE

> **LEAF**
> Ch 3, 2 dc in third ch from hook.

## SQUARE (Make 63)

**Rnd 1 (Right side):** With Pink, ch 2, 8 sc in second ch from hook; join with slip st to first sc.

*Note:* Loop a short piece of yarn around any stitch to mark Rnd 1 as **right** side.

**Rnd 2:** Ch 1, sc in same st, ch 3, skip next sc, ★ sc in next sc, ch 3, skip next sc; repeat from ★ 2 times **more**; join with slip st to first sc: 4 ch-3 sps.

**Rnd 3:** (Slip st, ch 1, 5 dc, ch 1, slip st) in first ch-3 sp **(Petal made)** and in each ch-3 sp around; do **not** join: 4 Petals.

**Rnd 4:** Ch 2; working **behind** Petals and in skipped sc on Rnd 1, (sc in next sc, ch 4) around; join with slip st to first sc: 4 ch-4 sps.

**Rnd 5:** (Slip st, ch 1, 7 dc, ch 1, slip st) in first ch-4 sp **(Petal made)** and in each ch-4 sp around; do **not** join: 4 Petals.

**Rnd 6:** Ch 3; working **behind** Petals and in ch-4 sps on Rnd 4, skip first 3 dc on Rnd 5, sc in sp **before** next dc, ch 4, ★ skip next 7 dc on Rnd 5, sc in sp **before** next dc, ch 4; repeat from ★ 2 times **more**; join with slip st to first sc, finish off: 4 ch-4 sps.

**Rnd 7:** With **right** side facing, join Green with sc in any ch-4 sp *(see Joining With Sc, page 126)*; ch 4, sc in same sp, work Leaf, sc in next sc, work Leaf, ★ (sc, ch 4, sc) in next ch-4 sp, work Leaf, sc in next sc, work Leaf; repeat from ★ 2 times **more**; join with slip st to first sc, finish off: 4 ch-4 sps and 8 Leaves.

**Rnd 8:** With **right** side facing, join White with slip st in any ch-4 sp; ch 6 **(counts as first dc plus ch 3, now and throughout)**, dc in same sp, ★ † ch 1, working **behind** next Leaf, dc in ch-4 sp on Rnd 6 to **left** of sc, ch 1, sc in next sc, ch 1, working **behind** next Leaf, dc in ch-4 sp on Rnd 6 to **right** of sc, ch 1 †, (dc, ch 3, dc) in next ch-4 sp; repeat from ★ 2 times **more**, then repeat from † to † once; join with slip st to first dc: 20 sts and 20 sps.

**Rnd 9:** Ch 4 **(counts as first dc plus ch 1, now and throughout)**, (dc, ch 3, dc) in next corner ch-3 sp, ch 1, dc in next dc, ch 1, ★ (skip next ch, dc in next st, ch 1) across to next corner ch-3 sp, (dc, ch 3, dc) in corner ch-3 sp, ch 1, dc in next dc, ch 1; repeat from ★ 2 times **more**, skip next ch, (dc in next st, ch 1, skip next ch) across; join with slip st to first dc: 28 dc and 28 sps.

**Rnd 10:** Ch 3, dc in next ch-1 sp and in next dc, ★ † (2 dc, ch 3, 2 dc) in next corner ch-3 sp, dc in next dc and in next ch-1 sp, dc in next dc †, (ch 1, skip next ch, dc in next dc) 4 times, dc in next ch-1 sp and in next dc; repeat from ★ 2 times **more**, then repeat from † to † once, ch 1, skip next ch, (dc in next dc, ch 1, skip next ch) 3 times; join with slip st to first dc, finish off: 52 dc and 20 sps.

## ASSEMBLY

Using White and working through both loops, whipstitch Squares together *(Fig. 26b, page 127)*, forming 7 vertical strips of 9 Squares each, beginning in center ch of first corner and ending in center ch of next corner; whipstitch strips together in same manner.

## EDGING

**Rnd 1 (Eyelet rnd):** With **right** side facing, join White with slip st in any corner ch-3 sp; ch 6, dc in same sp, ★ † ch 1, dc in next dc, ch 1, (skip next dc, dc in next dc, ch 1) twice, (dc in next dc, ch 1) 4 times, (skip next dc, dc in next dc, ch 1) twice, [dc in next joining, ch 1, dc in next dc, ch 1, (skip next dc, dc in next dc, ch 1) twice, (dc in next dc, ch 1) 4 times, (skip next dc, dc in next dc, ch 1) twice] across to next corner ch-3 sp †, (dc, ch 3, dc) in corner ch-3 sp; repeat from ★ 2 times **more**, then repeat from † to † once; join with slip st to first dc, finish off: 324 dc and 324 sps.

**Rnd 2:** With **right** side facing, join Pink with slip st in any corner ch-3 sp; ch 4, (dc, ch 1) 3 times in same sp, ★ (dc, ch 1) twice in each dc across to next corner ch-3 sp, (dc, ch 1) 4 times in corner ch-3 sp; repeat from ★ 2 times **more**, (dc, ch 1) twice in each dc across; join with slip st to first dc: 664 dc and 664 ch-1 sps.

**Rnds 3 and 4:** Ch 4, (dc in next dc, ch 1) around; join with slip st to first dc.
Finish off.

**Rnd 5:** With **right** side facing, join Green with slip st in same st as joining; ch 3, (slip st in next dc, ch 3) around; join with slip st to first slip st, finish off.

Working across **length** of Afghan, weave a 54" length of ribbon through Eyelet rnd; repeat on opposite side.
Working across **width** of Afghan, weave a 45" length of ribbon through Eyelet rnd; repeat on opposite side.
Tie ribbons in a bow at each corner and trim as desired.

# SPRING GARDEN

*Worked in brushed acrylic yarn reflecting spring tones,*
*this breezy afghan is super soft. An eyelet-look floral pattern*
*and rows of popcorn stitches accent the lovely wrap.*

**Finished Size:** 48" x 65"

## MATERIALS
Worsted Weight Brushed Acrylic Yarn:
Pastel Variegated - 36 ounces,
(1,020 grams, 2,775 yards)
Lavender - 3¹/2 ounces, (100 grams, 270 yards)
Crochet hook, size I (5.50 mm) **or** size needed for gauge
Yarn needle

**GAUGE:** Each Strip = 7¹/2" wide and 6 rows = 3"

## STITCH GUIDE

> **POPCORN**
> Work 5 hdc in st indicated, drop loop from hook, insert hook in first hdc of 5-hdc group, hook dropped loop and draw through *(Fig. 14, page 122).*
> **V-ST**
> (Dc, ch 1, dc) in st or sp indicated.

## STRIP (Make 6)
With Pastel Variegated, ch 27 **loosely.**

**Row 1** (Right side)**:** Work Popcorn in fourth ch from hook **(3 skipped chs count as first dc)**, dc in next ch, ch 1, skip next ch, work V-St in next ch, (ch 1, skip next ch, dc in next 6 chs) twice, ch 1, skip next ch, work V-St in next ch, ch 1, skip next ch, dc in next ch, work Popcorn in next ch, dc in last ch: 22 sts and 7 ch-1 sps.

*Note:* Loop a short piece of yarn around any stitch to mark Row 1 as **right** side and bottom edge.

**Row 2:** Ch 3 **(counts as first dc, now and throughout)**, turn; dc in next 2 sts, ch 1, skip next ch-1 sp, work V-St in next ch-1 sp, ch 1, skip next dc, dc in next 4 dc, ch 3, sc in next ch-1 sp, ch 3, skip next 2 dc, dc in next 4 dc, ch 1, skip next ch-1 sp, work V-St in next ch-1 sp, ch 1, dc in last 3 sts: 19 sts and 8 sps.

**Row 3:** Ch 3, turn; work Popcorn in next dc, dc in next dc, ch 1, skip next ch-1 sp, work V-St in next ch-1 sp, ch 1, skip next dc, dc in next 2 dc, ch 3, (sc in next ch-3 sp, ch 3) twice, skip next 2 dc, dc in next 2 dc, ch 1, skip next ch-1 sp, work V-St in next ch-1 sp, ch 1, skip next dc, dc in next dc, work Popcorn in next dc, dc in last dc: 16 sts and 9 sps.

**Row 4:** Ch 3, turn; dc in next 2 sts, ch 1, skip next ch-1 sp, work V-St in next ch-1 sp, ch 1, skip next dc, dc in next 2 dc, 2 dc in next ch-3 sp, ch 3, sc in next ch-3 sp, ch 3, 2 dc in next ch-3 sp, dc in next 2 dc, ch 1, skip next ch-1 sp, work V-St in next ch-1 sp, ch 1, dc in last 3 sts: 19 sts and 8 sps.

**Row 5:** Ch 3, turn; work Popcorn in next dc, dc in next dc, ch 1, skip next ch-1 sp, work V-St in next ch-1 sp, ch 1, skip next dc, dc in next 4 dc, 2 dc in next ch-3 sp, ch 1, 2 dc in next ch-3 sp, dc in next 4 dc, ch 1, skip next ch-1 sp, work V-St in next ch-1 sp, ch 1, skip next dc, dc in next dc, work Popcorn in next dc, dc in last dc: 22 sts and 7 ch-1 sps.

**Row 6:** Ch 3, turn; dc in next 2 sts, ch 1, skip next ch-1 sp, work V-St in next ch-1 sp, ch 1, skip next dc, dc in next 6 dc, dc in next ch-1 sp and in next 6 dc, ch 1, skip next ch-1 sp, work V-St in next ch-1 sp, ch 1, dc in last 3 sts: 23 dc and 6 ch-1 sps.

**Row 7:** Ch 3, turn; work Popcorn in next dc, dc in next dc, ch 1, skip next ch-1 sp, work V-St in next ch-1 sp, (ch 1, skip next dc, dc in next 6 dc) twice, ch 1, skip next ch-1 sp, work V-St in next ch-1 sp, ch 1, skip next dc, dc in next dc, work Popcorn in next dc, dc in last dc: 22 sts and 7 ch-1 sps.

**Rows 8-127:** Repeat Rows 2-7, 20 times.
Do **not** finish off.

## BORDER
Ch 1, do **not** turn; work 253 sc evenly spaced across end of rows; working in free loops of beginning ch *(Fig. 25b, page 126)*, 3 sc in first ch, sc in next 23 chs, 3 sc in next ch; work 253 sc evenly spaced across end of rows; working across Row 127, 3 sc in first dc, sc in next 2 sts, skip next ch-1 sp, sc in next dc and in next ch-1 sp, sc in next dc, skip next ch-1 sp, sc in next 6 dc, sc in next ch-1 sp and in next 6 dc, skip next ch-1 sp, sc in next dc, sc in next ch-1 sp and in next dc, skip next ch-1 sp, sc in next 2 sts, 3 sc in last dc; join with slip st to first sc, finish off: 564 sc.

## ASSEMBLY
Place two Strips with **wrong** sides together and bottom edges at the same end. Join Lavender with sc in center sc of first corner on **first Strip** *(see Joining With Sc, page 126)*; ch 1, sc in center sc of first corner on **previous Strip**

*(Fig. 21, page 124)*, ★ ch 1, skip next sc on **first Strip**, sc in next sc, ch 1, skip next sc on **previous Strip**, sc in next sc; repeat from ★ across working last sc in center sc of next corner on **previous Strip**; finish off.

Join remaining Strips in the same manner, always working in same direction.

# EDGING

**Rnd 1:** With **wrong** side facing, join Lavender with sc in any sc; sc evenly around working 3 sc in center sc of each corner and working an even number of sc; join with slip st to first sc.

**Rnd 2:** Ch 1, turn; sc in same st, ch 2, skip next sc, (sc in next sc, ch 2, skip next sc) around; join with slip st to first sc, finish off.

# RING AROUND THE ROSES

*On this flowering fancy, bars of sweet rosebuds and small granny squares encircle larger blocks, which feature lavish full blooms. Double crochets and cluster stitches provide a three-dimensional effect for the roses.*

Finished Size: 49" x 67"

## MATERIALS
Worsted Weight Yarn:
Ecru - 24 ounces, (680 grams, 1,580 yards)
Rose - 10 ounces, (280 grams, 660 yards)
Green - 11 ounces, (310 grams, 725 yards)
Crochet hook, size I (5.50 mm) **or** size needed for gauge
Yarn needle

GAUGE: Each Large Square = 6"

## STITCH GUIDE

> **CLUSTER**
> ★ YO twice, insert hook in third ch from hook, YO and pull up a loop, (YO and draw through 2 loops on hook) twice; repeat from ★ 2 times **more**, YO and draw through all 4 loops on hook *(Figs. 16a & b, page 123)*.

## LARGE SQUARE (Make 35)
**Rnd 1 (Right side):** With Rose, ch 2, 8 sc in second ch from hook; join with slip st to first sc.
*Note:* Loop a short piece of yarn around any stitch to mark Rnd 1 as **right** side.
**Rnd 2:** Ch 1, sc in same st, ch 3, skip next sc, (sc in next sc, ch 3, skip next sc) around; join with slip st to first sc: 4 ch-3 sps.
**Rnd 3:** (Slip st, ch 2, 4 dc, ch 2, slip st) in first ch-3 sp **(Petal made)** and in each ch-3 sp around; join with slip st to first slip st: 4 Petals.
**Rnd 4:** Ch 2, working **behind** Petals and in skipped sc on Rnd 1, sc in first sc, ch 4, (sc in next sc, ch 4) around; join with slip st to first sc: 4 ch-4 sps.
**Rnd 5:** (Slip st, ch 2, 8 dc, ch 2, slip st) in first ch-4 sp **(Petal made)** and in each ch-4 sp around; join with slip st to first slip st: 4 Petals.
**Rnd 6:** Ch 3, working **behind** Petals and in ch-4 sps on Rnd 4, sc in first ch-4 sp **between** center 2 dc of Petal, ch 5, (sc in next ch-4 sp **between** center 2 dc of Petal, ch 5) around; join with slip st to first sc, finish off: 4 ch-5 sps.
**Rnd 7:** With **right** side facing, join Ecru with sc in same st as joining *(see Joining With Sc, page 126)*; ch 1, (hdc, dc, ch 3, dc, hdc) in next ch-5 sp, ch 1, ★ sc in next sc, ch 1, (hdc, dc, ch 3, dc, hdc) in next ch-5 sp, ch 1; repeat from ★ around; join with slip st to first sc: 12 sps.

**Rnd 8:** Ch 3 **(counts as first dc, now and throughout)**, 2 dc in same st, ch 1, (3 dc, ch 3, 3 dc) in next ch-3 sp, ch 1, ★ 3 dc in next sc, ch 1, (3 dc, ch 3, 3 dc) in next ch-3 sp, ch 1; repeat from ★ around; join with slip st to first dc, finish off.
**Rnd 9:** With **right** side facing, join Green with slip st in any ch-3 sp; ch 3, (2 dc, ch 3, 3 dc) in same sp, ch 1, (3 dc in next ch-1 sp, ch 1) across to next ch-3 sp, ★ (3 dc, ch 3, 3 dc) in ch-3 sp, ch 1, (3 dc in next ch-1 sp, ch 1) across to next ch-3 sp; repeat from ★ around; join with slip st to first dc, finish off: 16 sps.
**Rnd 10:** With Ecru, repeat Rnd 9: 20 sps.

## SMALL SQUARE (Make 48)
**Rnd 1 (Right side):** With Green, ch 4, 2 dc in fourth ch from hook, ch 3, (3 dc in same ch, ch 3) 3 times; join with slip st to top of beginning ch-4, finish off: 4 ch-3 sps.
*Note:* Mark Rnd 1 as **right** side.
**Rnd 2:** With **right** side facing, join Ecru with slip st in any ch-3 sp; ch 3, (2 dc, ch 3, 3 dc) in same sp, ch 1, ★ (3 dc, ch 3, 3 dc) in next ch-3 sp, ch 1; repeat from ★ around; join with slip st to first dc, finish off: 8 sps.

## BAR (Make 82)
**Foundation Row (Wrong side):** With Rose, (ch 4, work Cluster) 3 times, ch 1; finish off: 3 Clusters (3³/₄").
*Note:* Mark **back** of last Cluster made as **right** side.
**Rnd 1:** With **right** side facing, join Green with slip st in last ch made; ch 3, 2 dc in same ch, (ch 3, 3 dc in same ch) twice, ch 1; working in ch between Clusters, (3 dc in next ch between Clusters, ch 1) twice, 3 dc in last ch, (ch 3, 3 dc in same ch) twice, ch 1; working in free loops of each ch on Foundation Row, (3 dc in next ch, ch 1) twice; join with slip st to first dc, finish off: 10 sps.
**Rnd 2:** With **right** side facing and holding Bar vertically, join Ecru with slip st in top right ch-3 sp; ch 3, (2 dc, ch 3, 3 dc) in same sp, ch 1, (3 dc, ch 3, 3 dc) in next ch-3 sp, ch 1, (3 dc in next ch-1 sp, ch 1) 3 times, [(3 dc, ch 3, 3 dc) in next ch-3 sp, ch 1] twice, (3 dc in next ch-1 sp, ch 1) 3 times; join with slip st to first dc, finish off: 14 sps.

Continued on page 28.

## ASSEMBLY

With Ecru, using Placement Diagram as a guide, and working through both loops, whipstitch Squares and Bars together *(Fig. 26b, page 127)*, forming 5 vertical strips of 7 Large Squares and 8 Bars, then forming 6 vertical strips of 8 Small Squares and 7 Bars, beginning in center ch of first corner ch-3 and ending in center ch of next corner ch-3; whipstitch strips together in same manner.

## EDGING

**Rnd 1:** With **right** side facing, join Ecru with sc in any corner ch-3 sp; ch 2, sc in same sp, ★ † ch 1, skip next dc, sc in next dc, ch 1, sc in next ch-1 sp, ch 1, skip next dc, sc in next dc, ch 1, [(sc in next ch-sp, ch 1) twice, skip next dc, sc in next dc, ch 1, (sc in next ch-1 sp, ch 1, skip next dc, sc in next dc, ch 1) 4 times, (sc in next ch-sp, ch 1) twice, skip next dc, sc in next dc, ch 1, sc in next ch-1 sp, ch 1, skip next dc, sc in next dc, ch 1] across to next corner ch-3 sp †, (sc, ch 2, sc) in ch-3 sp; repeat from ★ 2 times **more**, then repeat from † to † once; join with slip st to first sc.
**Rnd 2:** Slip st in first ch-2 sp, ch 1, (sc, ch 2, sc) in same sp, ch 1, (sc in next ch-1 sp, ch 1) across to next ch-2 sp, ★ (sc, ch 2, sc) in ch-2 sp, ch 1, (sc in next ch-1 sp, ch 1) across to next ch-2 sp; repeat from ★ around; join with slip st to first sc.

**Rnd 3:** (Slip st, ch 1) twice in first ch-2 sp, (slip st in next ch-1 sp, ch 1) across to next ch-2 sp, ★ (slip st, ch 1) twice in ch-2 sp, (slip st in next ch-1 sp, ch 1) across to next ch-2 sp; repeat from ★ around; join with slip st to first slip st, finish off.

### PLACEMENT DIAGRAM

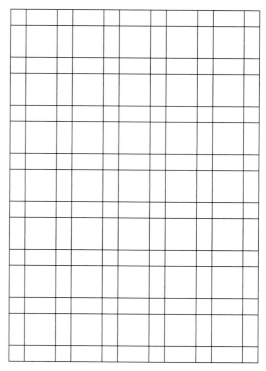

# DELIGHTFUL DAFFODILS

*This bed of sunny daffodils will add a splash of color wherever it's used!*
*A placement diagram makes assembling this springtime afghan extra easy.*

**Finished Size:** 51" x 63"

## MATERIALS
Worsted Weight Yarn:
  Yellow - 24 ounces, (680 grams, 1,580 yards)
  Green - 17 ounces, (480 grams, 1,120 yards)
  Ecru - 7 ounces, (200 grams, 460 yards)
Crochet hook, size I (5.50 mm) **or** size needed for gauge
Yarn needle

**GAUGE:** Each Small Square = 4¹/4"
Each Large Square = 8"

## STITCH GUIDE

**CLUSTER**
★ YO twice, insert hook in third ch from hook, YO and pull up a loop, (YO and draw through 2 loops on hook) twice; repeat from ★ 2 times **more**, YO and draw through all 4 loops on hook *(Figs. 16a & b, page 123)*.

Continued on page 30.

# LARGE SQUARE (Make 20)

**Rnd 1 (Right side):** With Yellow, ch 2, 6 sc in second ch from hook; join with slip st to first sc.

*Note:* Loop a short piece of yarn around any stitch to mark Rnd 1 as **right** side.

**Rnd 2:** Ch 1, 2 sc in same st and in each sc around; join with slip st to Front Loop Only of first sc (*Fig. 24, page 126*): 12 sc.

**Rnd 3:** Ch 1, sc in Front Loop Only of same st and in each sc around; join with slip st to both loops of first sc.

**Rnd 4:** Ch 1, (slip st in both loops of next sc, ch 1) around; join with slip st to base of beginning ch-1, finish off.

**Rnd 5:** With **right** side facing and working in free loops on Rnd 2 (*Fig. 25a, page 126*), join Yellow with sc in any sc (*see Joining With Sc, page 126*); ch 1, in same st work [dc, ch 1, tr, ch 3, tr, ch 1, dc, ch 1, sc (**Petal made**)], ch 1, skip next sc, ★ in next sc work [sc, ch 1, dc, ch 1, tr, ch 3, tr, ch 1, dc, ch 1, sc (**Petal made**)], ch 1, skip next sc; repeat from ★ around; join with slip st to first sc, finish off: 6 Petals.

**Rnd 6:** With **right** side facing, join Green with sc in any ch-1 sp between Petals; ch 4, working **behind** Petals, (sc in ch-1 sp **before** next Petal, ch 4) around; join with slip st to first sc: 6 ch-4 sps.

**Rnd 7:** Ch 1, sc in same st, ch 1, † sc in next ch-4 sp, ch 6, sc in next sc, ch 1, sc in next ch-4 sp, ch 1, sc in next sc, ch 6, sc in next ch-4 sp, ch 1 †, sc in next sc, ch 1, repeat from † to † once; join with slip st to first sc: 12 sps.

**Rnd 8:** Ch 3 (**counts as first dc, now and throughout**), 2 dc in same st, ch 1, † dc in next ch-6 sp, sc in back ridge of center ch on Petal **below** (*Fig. 2c, page 120*), (dc, ch 3, 3 dc) in same sp as last dc made, ch 1, skip next sc, dc in next sc, sc in back ridge of center ch of next Petal **below**, dc in same sc as last dc made, ch 1, (3 dc, ch 3, dc) in next ch-6 sp, sc in back ridge of center ch on next Petal **below**, dc in same sp as last dc made, ch 1 †, skip next sc, 3 dc in next sc, ch 1, repeat from † to † once; join with slip st to first dc.

**Rnd 9:** Slip st in next 2 dc and in next ch-1 sp, ch 3, 2 dc in same sp, ch 1, (3 dc, ch 3, 3 dc) in next ch-3 sp, ch 1, ★ (3 dc in next ch-1 sp, ch 1) twice, (3 dc, ch 3, 3 dc) in next ch-3 sp, ch 1; repeat from ★ 2 times **more**, 3 dc in last ch-1 sp, ch 1; join with slip st to first dc, finish off: 16 sps.

**Rnd 10:** With **right** side facing, join Ecru with slip st in any ch-3 sp; ch 3, (2 dc, ch 3, 3 dc) in same sp, ch 1, (3 dc in next ch-1 sp, ch 1) across to next ch-3 sp, ★ (3 dc, ch 3, 3 dc) in ch-3 sp, ch 1, (3 dc in next ch-1 sp, ch 1) across to next ch-3 sp; repeat from ★ around; join with slip st to first dc, finish off: 20 sps.

**Rnd 11:** With Green, repeat Rnd 10: 24 sps.

**Rnd 12:** With Yellow, repeat Rnd 10: 28 sps.

# SMALL SQUARE (Make 30)

**Rnd 1 (Right side):** With Ecru, ch 4, 2 dc in fourth ch from hook, ch 3, (3 dc in same ch, ch 3) 3 times; join with slip st to top of beginning ch-4, finish off: 4 ch-3 sps.

*Note:* Mark Rnd 1 as **right** side.

**Rnd 2:** With **right** side facing, join Green with slip st in any ch-3 sp; ch 3, (2 dc, ch 3, 3 dc) in same sp, ch 1, ★ (3 dc, ch 3, 3 dc) in next ch-3 sp, ch 1; repeat from ★ around; join with slip st to first dc, finish off: 8 sps.

**Rnd 3:** With **right** side facing, join Yellow with slip st in any ch-3 sp; ch 3, (2 dc, ch 3, 3 dc) in same sp, ch 1, 3 dc in next ch-1 sp, ch 1, ★ (3 dc, ch 3, 3 dc) in next ch-3 sp, ch 1, 3 dc in next ch-1 sp, ch 1; repeat from ★ around; join with slip st to first dc, finish off: 12 sps.

# BAR (Make 49)

**Foundation Row (Wrong side):** With Yellow, (ch 4, work Cluster) 4 times, ch 1; finish off: 4 Clusters (5").

*Note:* Mark **back** of last Cluster made as **right** side.

**Rnd 1:** With **right** side facing, join Ecru with slip st in last ch made; ch 3, 2 dc in same ch, (ch 3, 3 dc in same ch) twice; ch 1, working in ch between Clusters, (3 dc in next ch, ch 1) 3 times, 3 dc in last ch, (ch 3, 3 dc in same ch) twice, ch 1; working in free loops of each ch on Foundation Row, (3 dc in next ch, ch 1) 3 times; join with slip st to first dc, finish off: 12 sps.

**Rnd 2:** With **right** side facing and holding Bar vertically, join Green with slip st in top right ch-3 sp; ch 3, (2 dc, ch 3, 3 dc) in same sp, ch 1, (3 dc, ch 3, 3 dc) in next ch-3 sp, ch 1, (3 dc in next ch-1 sp, ch 1) 4 times, [(3 dc, ch 3, 3 dc) in next ch-3 sp, ch 1] twice, (3 dc in next ch-1 sp, ch 1) across; join with slip st to first dc, finish off: 16 sps.

**Rnd 3:** With **right** side facing and holding Bar vertically, join Yellow with slip st in top right ch-3 sp; ch 3, (2 dc, ch 3, 3 dc) in same sp, † ch 1, 3 dc in next ch-1 sp, ch 1, (3 dc, ch 3, 3 dc) in next ch-3 sp, ch 1, (3 dc in next ch-1 sp, ch 1) across to next ch-3 sp †, (3 dc, ch 3, 3 dc) in ch-3 sp, repeat from † to † once; join with slip st to first dc, finish off: 20 sps.

# ASSEMBLY

With Yellow, using Placement Diagram as a guide, and working through both loops, whipstitch Squares and Bars together *(Fig. 26b, page 127)*, forming 4 vertical strips of 5 Large Squares and 6 Bars, then forming 5 vertical strips of 6 Small Squares and 5 Bars, beginning in center ch of first corner ch-3 and ending in center ch of next corner ch-3; whipstitch strips together in same manner.

# EDGING

**Rnd 1:** With **right** side facing, join Yellow with sc in any corner ch-3 sp; ch 2, sc in same sp, ★ † ch 1, skip next dc, sc in next dc, ch 1, (sc in next ch-1 sp, ch 1, skip next dc, sc in next dc, ch 1) twice, [(sc in next ch-sp, ch 1) twice, skip next dc, sc in next dc, ch 1, (sc in next ch-1 sp, ch 1, skip next dc, sc in next dc, ch 1) 6 times, (sc in next ch-sp, ch 1) twice, skip next dc, sc in next dc, ch 1, (sc in next ch-1 sp, ch 1, skip next dc, sc in next dc, ch 1) twice] across to next corner ch-3 sp †, (sc, ch 2, sc) in ch-3 sp; repeat from ★ 2 times **more**, then repeat from † to † once; join with slip st to first sc.

**Rnd 2:** Slip st in first ch-2 sp, ch 1, (sc, ch 2, sc) in same sp, ch 1, (sc in next ch-1 sp, ch 1) across to next ch-2 sp, ★ (sc, ch 2, sc) in ch-2 sp, ch 1, (sc in next ch-1 sp, ch 1) across to next ch-2 sp; repeat from ★ around; join with slip st to first sc.

**Rnd 3:** (Slip st, ch 1) twice in first ch-2 sp, (slip st in next ch-1 sp, ch 1) across to next ch-2 sp, ★ (slip st, ch 1) twice in ch-2 sp, (slip st in next ch-1 sp, ch 1) across to next ch-2 sp; repeat from ★ around; join with slip st to first slip st, finish off.

## PLACEMENT DIAGRAM

# HOME
## is where the heart is

Home is always where our hearts long to be. Even if only in our thoughts, we go there to treasure memories of time spent with loved ones. Heart-embellished afghans that convey the warmth of home make up this charming collection. From soft and cuddly baby wraps to throws with classic lines or country flair, there's a homemade afghan just for you — and everyone you hold close to your heart!

# IN LOVE WITH LACE

*Cluster-stitch hearts are sure to capture your fancy on this lacy afghan of chain stitches and spaces. A simple scalloped edging finishes the lovely blanket.*

**Finished Size:** 49" x 70"

## MATERIALS
Worsted Weight Yarn:
44¹/₂ ounces, (1,260 grams, 3,050 yards)
Crochet hook, size I (5.50 mm) **or** size needed for gauge

**GAUGE:** In pattern, sc, (ch 4, sc) 5 times = 4¹/₂" and
9 rows = 4"

**Gauge Swatch:** 17¹/₄"w x 5"h
Ch 62 **loosely.**
Work same as Rows 1-12.
Finish off.

## STITCH GUIDE

> **CLUSTER**
> YO twice, insert hook in **next** sc, YO and pull up a loop, (YO and draw through 2 loops on hook) twice, ★ YO twice, insert hook in **same** st, YO and pull up a loop, (YO and draw through 2 loops on hook) twice; repeat from ★ 2 times **more**, YO and draw through all 5 loops on hook, ch 1 to close. Push Cluster to **right** side (*Figs. 16a & b, page 123*).

Ch 170 **loosely.**
**Row 1 (Right side):** Sc in second ch from hook, ★ ch 4, skip next 2 chs, sc in next ch; repeat from ★ across: 57 sc and 56 ch-4 sps.
**Row 2:** Ch 4 **(counts as first dc plus ch 1, now and throughout),** turn; sc in first ch-4 sp, (ch 4, sc in next ch-4 sp) 3 times, ch 1, work Cluster, sc in next ch-4 sp, ★ (ch 4, sc in next ch-4 sp) 11 times, ch 1, work Cluster, sc in next ch-4 sp; repeat from ★ across to last 3 ch-4 sps, (ch 4, sc in next ch-4 sp) 3 times, ch 1, dc in last sc: 5 Clusters and 50 ch-4 sps.
**Row 3:** Ch 1, turn; sc in first dc, ch 4, skip next ch-1 sp, (sc in next ch-4 sp, ch 4) 3 times, sc in next Cluster, ch 4, ★ (sc in next ch-4 sp, ch 4) 11 times, sc in next Cluster, ch 4; repeat from ★ across to last 3 ch-4 sps, (sc in next ch-4 sp, ch 4) 3 times, skip next ch-1 sp, sc in last dc: 57 sc and 56 ch-4 sps.
**Row 4:** Ch 4, turn; sc in first ch-4 sp, (ch 4, sc in next ch-4 sp) twice, (ch 1, work Cluster, sc in next ch-4 sp) 3 times, ★ (ch 4, sc in next ch-4 sp) 9 times, (ch 1, work Cluster, sc in next ch-4 sp) 3 times; repeat from ★ across to last 2 ch-4 sps, (ch 4, sc in next ch-4 sp) twice, ch 1, dc in last sc: 15 Clusters and 40 ch-4 sps.

**Row 5:** Ch 1, turn; sc in first dc, ch 4, skip next ch-1 sp, (sc in next ch-4 sp, ch 4) twice, (sc in next Cluster, ch 4) 3 times, ★ (sc in next ch-4 sp, ch 4) 9 times, (sc in next Cluster, ch 4) 3 times; repeat from ★ across to last 2 ch-4 sps, (sc in next ch-4 sp, ch 4) twice, skip next ch-1 sp, sc in last dc: 57 sc and 56 ch-4 sps.
**Row 6:** Ch 4, turn; sc in first ch-4 sp, ch 4, sc in next ch-4 sp, (ch 1, work Cluster, sc in next ch-4 sp) 5 times, ★ (ch 4, sc in next ch-4 sp) 7 times, (ch 1, work Cluster, sc in next ch-4 sp) 5 times; repeat from ★ across to last ch-4 sp, ch 4, sc in last ch-4 sp, ch 1, dc in last sc: 25 Clusters and 30 ch-4 sps.
**Row 7:** Ch 1, turn; sc in first dc, ch 4, skip next ch-1 sp, sc in next ch-4 sp, ch 4, (sc in next Cluster, ch 4) 5 times, ★ (sc in next ch-4 sp, ch 4) 7 times, (sc in next Cluster, ch 4) 5 times; repeat from ★ across to last ch-4 sp, sc in last ch-4 sp, ch 4, skip next ch-1 sp, sc in last dc: 57 sc and 56 ch-4 sps.
**Row 8:** Ch 4, turn; sc in first ch-4 sp, (ch 1, work Cluster, sc in next ch-4 sp) 7 times, ★ (ch 4, sc in next ch-4 sp) 5 times, (ch 1, work Cluster, sc in next ch-4 sp) 7 times; repeat from ★ across to last sc, ch 1, dc in last sc: 35 Clusters and 20 ch-4 sps.
**Row 9:** Ch 1, turn; sc in first dc, ch 4, skip next ch-1 sp, (sc in next Cluster, ch 4) 7 times, ★ (sc in next ch-4 sp, ch 4) 5 times, (sc in next Cluster, ch 4) 7 times; repeat from ★ across to last dc, sc in last dc: 57 sc and 56 ch-4 sps.
**Rows 10 and 11:** Repeat Rows 8 and 9.
**Row 12:** Ch 4, turn; sc in first ch-4 sp, ch 4, sc in next ch-4 sp, (ch 1, work Cluster, sc in next ch-4 sp) twice, ch 4, sc in next ch-4 sp, (ch 1, work Cluster, sc in next ch-4 sp) twice, ★ (ch 4, sc in next ch-4 sp) 3 times, ch 1, work Cluster, sc in next ch-4 sp, (ch 4, sc in next ch-4 sp) 3 times, (ch 1, work Cluster, sc in next ch-4 sp) twice; repeat from ★ across to last ch-4 sp, ch 4, sc in last ch-4 sp, ch 1, dc in last sc: 24 Clusters and 31 ch-4 sps.
**Row 13:** Ch 1, turn; sc in first dc, ch 4, skip next ch-1 sp, [sc in next ch-4 sp, ch 4, (sc in next Cluster, ch 4) twice] 2 times, ★ (sc in next ch-4 sp, ch 4) 3 times, sc in next Cluster, ch 4, (sc in next ch-4 sp, ch 4) 3 times, (sc in next Cluster, ch 4) twice, sc in next ch-4 sp, ch 4, (sc in next Cluster, ch 4) twice; repeat from ★ across to last ch-4 sp, sc in last ch-4 sp, ch 4, skip next ch-1 sp, sc in last dc: 57 sc and 56 ch-4 sps.
**Row 14:** Ch 4, turn; sc in first ch-4 sp, (ch 4, sc in next ch-4 sp) 8 times, (ch 1, work Cluster, sc in next ch-4 sp) 3 times, ★ (ch 4, sc in next ch-4 sp) 9 times, (ch 1, work Cluster, sc in next ch-4 sp) 3 times; repeat from ★ across to last 8 ch-4 sps, (ch 4, sc in next ch-4 sp) 8 times, ch 1, dc in last sc: 12 Clusters and 43 ch-4 sps.

**Row 15:** Ch 1, turn; sc in first dc, ch 4, skip next ch-1 sp, (sc in next ch-4 sp, ch 4) 8 times, (sc in next Cluster, ch 4) 3 times, ★ (sc in next ch-4 sp, ch 4) 9 times, (sc in next Cluster, ch 4) 3 times; repeat from ★ across to last 8 ch-4 sps, (sc in next ch-4 sp, ch 4) 8 times, skip next ch-1 sp, sc in last dc: 57 sc and 56 ch-4 sps.

**Row 16:** Ch 4, turn; sc in first ch-4 sp, (ch 4, sc in next ch-4 sp) 7 times, ★ (ch 1, work Cluster, sc in next ch-4 sp) 5 times, (ch 4, sc in next ch-4 sp) 7 times; repeat from ★ across to last sc, ch 1, dc in last sc: 20 Clusters and 35 ch-4 sps.

**Row 17:** Ch 1, turn; sc in first dc, ch 4, skip next ch-1 sp, (sc in next ch-4 sp, ch 4) 7 times, ★ (sc in next Cluster, ch 4) 5 times, (sc in next ch-4 sp, ch 4) 7 times; repeat from ★ across to last dc, sc in last dc: 57 sc and 56 ch-4 sps.

**Row 18:** Ch 4, turn; sc in first ch-4 sp, (ch 4, sc in next ch-4 sp) 6 times, (ch 1, work Cluster, sc in next ch-4 sp) 7 times, ★ (ch 4, sc in next ch-4 sp) 5 times, (ch 1, work Cluster, sc in next ch-4 sp) 7 times; repeat from ★ across to last 6 ch-4 sps, (ch 4, sc in next ch-4 sp) 6 times, ch 1, dc in last sc: 28 Clusters and 27 ch-4 sps.

Continued on page 36.

**Row 19:** Ch 1, turn; sc in first dc, ch 4, skip next ch-1 sp, (sc in next ch-4 sp, ch 4) 6 times, (sc in next Cluster, ch 4) 7 times, ★ (sc in next ch-4 sp, ch 4) 5 times, (sc in next Cluster, ch 4) 7 times; repeat from ★ across to last 6 ch-4 sps, (sc in next ch-4 sp, ch 4) 6 times, skip next ch-1 sp, sc in last dc: 57 sc and 56 ch-4 sps.

**Rows 20 and 21:** Repeat Rows 18 and 19.

**Row 22:** Ch 4, turn; sc in first ch-4 sp, (ch 4, sc in next ch-4 sp) 3 times, ch 1, work Cluster, sc in next ch-4 sp, (ch 4, sc in next ch-4 sp) 3 times, ★ (ch 1, work Cluster, sc in next ch-4 sp) twice, ch 4, sc in next ch-4 sp, (ch 1, work Cluster, sc in next ch-4 sp) twice, (ch 4, sc in next ch-4 sp) 3 times, ch 1, work Cluster, sc in next ch-4 sp, (ch 4, sc in next ch-4 sp) 3 times; repeat from ★ across to last sc, ch 1, dc in last sc: 21 Clusters and 34 ch-4 sps.

**Row 23:** Ch 1, turn; sc in first dc, ch 4, skip next ch-1 sp, (sc in next ch-4 sp, ch 4) 3 times, sc in next Cluster, ch 4, (sc in next ch-4 sp, ch 4) 3 times, ★ (sc in next Cluster, ch 4) twice, sc in next ch-4 sp, ch 4, (sc in next Cluster, ch 4) twice, (sc in next ch-4 sp, ch 4) 3 times, sc in next Cluster, ch 4, (sc in next ch-4 sp, ch 4) 3 times; repeat from ★ across to last dc, sc in last dc: 57 sc and 56 ch-4 sps.

**Rows 24-151:** Repeat Rows 4-23, 6 times; then repeat Rows 4-11 once **more**: 57 sc and 56 ch-4 sps.

**Row 152:** Ch 4, turn; sc in first ch-4 sp, ch 4, sc in next ch-4 sp, (ch 1, work Cluster, sc in next ch-4 sp) twice, ch 4, sc in next ch-4 sp, (ch 1, work Cluster, sc in next ch-4 sp) twice, ★ (ch 4, sc in next ch-4 sp) 7 times, (ch 1, work Cluster, sc in next ch-4 sp) twice, ch 4, sc in next ch-4 sp, (ch 1, work Cluster, sc in next ch-4 sp) twice; repeat from ★ across to last ch-4 sp, ch 4, sc in last ch-4 sp, ch 1, dc in last sc: 20 Clusters and 35 ch-4 sps.

**Row 153:** Ch 1, turn; sc in first dc, ch 2, [sc in next ch-4 sp, ch 2, (sc in next Cluster, ch 2) twice] 2 times, ★ (sc in next ch-4 sp, ch 2) 7 times, (sc in next Cluster, ch 2) twice, sc in next ch-4 sp, ch 2, (sc in next Cluster, ch 2) twice; repeat from ★ across to last ch-4 sp, sc in last ch-4 sp, ch 2, sc in last dc; do **not** finish off: 57 sc and 56 ch-2 sps.

**Edging:** Ch 2, do **not** turn; (dc, ch 1, slip st, ch 2, dc) in last sc made on Row 153; working in end of rows, skip first row, [(slip st, ch 2, dc) in next row, skip next row] across to next corner; working in free loops of beginning ch (*Fig. 25b, page 126*), (slip st, ch 2, dc, ch 1, slip st, ch 2, 2 dc) in first ch, skip next 3 chs, (slip st, ch 2, 2 dc) in next ch, ★ skip next 2 chs, (slip st, ch 2, 2 dc) in next ch; repeat from ★ 53 times **more**, skip next ch, (slip st, ch 2, dc, ch 1, slip st, ch 2, dc) in next ch; working in end of rows, skip first row, [(slip st, ch 2, dc) in next row, skip next row] across to next corner; working across sc on Row 153, (slip st, ch 2, dc, ch 1, slip st, ch 2, 2 dc) in first sc, (slip st, ch 2, 2 dc) in next sc and in each sc across; join with slip st to base of beginning ch-2, finish off.

# CHAIN OF HEARTS

*Long double crochets worked in previous rows form an unbroken chain of hearts on this plush afghan. It will be a sentimental favorite year after year.*

**Finished Size:** 47" x 60"

**MATERIALS**
Worsted Weight Yarn:
49 ounces, (1,390 grams, 3,080 yards)
Crochet hook, size I (5.50 mm) **or** size needed for gauge

**GAUGE:** In pattern, 14 sts and 13 rows = 4"

**Gauge Swatch** 9"w x 4"h
Ch 32 **loosely.**
**Rows 1-13:** Work same as Afghan: 31 sts.

*Note:* Each row is worked across length of Afghan. When joining yarn and finishing off, always leave a 7" end to be worked into fringe.

## STITCH GUIDE

**LONG DOUBLE CROCHET** (*abbreviated LDC*)
YO, insert hook in free loop of sc one row **below** (*Fig. 25a, page 126*), YO and pull up a loop, (YO and draw through 2 loops on hook) twice (*Fig. 17, page 123*) (counts as one dc).

Ch 212 **loosely.**
**Row 1 (Right side):** Sc in second ch from hook and in each ch across; finish off: 211 sc.
*Note #1:* Loop a short piece of yarn around any stitch to mark Row 1 as **right** side.
*Note #2:* Work in Back Loops Only throughout (*Fig. 24, page 126*).
**Rows 2-4:** With **right** side facing, join yarn with slip st in first sc; ch 1, sc in each sc across; finish off.

**Row 5:** With **right** side facing, join yarn with slip st in first sc; ch 1, sc in first 9 sc, work LDC, skip sc behind dc **(now and throughout)**, (sc in next 11 sc, work LDC) across to last 9 sc, sc in last 9 sc; finish off: 17 dc.

**Row 6:** With **right** side facing, join yarn with slip st in first sc; ch 1, sc in first 8 sc, work LDC, sc in next dc, work LDC, ★ sc in next 9 sc, work LDC, sc in next dc, work LDC; repeat from ★ across to last 8 sc, sc in last 8 sc; finish off: 34 dc.

**Row 7:** With **right** side facing, join yarn with slip st in first sc; ch 1, sc in first 7 sc, ★ work LDC, sc in next 3 sts, work LDC, sc in next 7 sc; repeat from ★ across; finish off.

**Row 8:** With **right** side facing, join yarn with slip st in first sc; ch 1, sc in first 6 sc, work LDC, (sc in next 5 sts, work LDC) across to last 6 sc, sc in last 6 sc; finish off.

**Row 9:** With **right** side facing, join yarn with slip st in first sc; ch 1, sc in first 5 sc, work LDC, sc in next 7 sts, work LDC, ★ sc in next 3 sc, work LDC, sc in next 7 sts, work LDC; repeat from ★ across to last 5 sc, sc in last 5 sc; finish off.

**Row 10:** With **right** side facing, join yarn with slip st in first sc; ch 1, sc in first 4 sc, work LDC, sc in next 9 sts, work LDC, ★ sc in next sc, work LDC, sc in next 9 sts, work LDC; repeat from ★ across to last 4 sc, sc in last 4 sc; finish off.

Continued on page 38.

**Row 11:** With **right** side facing, join yarn with slip st in first sc; ch 1, sc in first 3 sc, work LDC, (sc in next 11 sts, work LDC) across to last 3 sc, sc in last 3 sc; finish off: 18 dc.

**Row 12:** With **right** side facing, join yarn with slip st in first sc; ch 1, sc in first 3 sc, dc around post of next dc *(Fig. 10, page 122)*, ★ sc in next 5 sc, work LDC, sc in next 5 sc, dc around post of next dc; repeat from ★ across to last 3 sc, sc in last 3 sc; finish off: 35 dc.

**Row 13:** With **right** side facing, join yarn with slip st in first sc; ch 1, sc in first 4 sts, work LDC, sc in next 3 sc, work LDC, ★ sc in next dc, work LDC, sc in next 3 sc, work LDC; repeat from ★ across to last 4 sts, sc in last 4 sts; finish off: 68 dc.

**Row 14:** With **right** side facing, join yarn with slip st in first sc; ch 1, sc in first 5 sts, work 3 LDC, (sc in next 3 sts, work 3 LDC) across to last 5 sts, sc in last 5 sts; finish off: 102 dc.

**Rows 15-17:** With **right** side facing, join yarn with slip st in first sc; ch 1, sc in each st across; finish off: 211 sc. Repeat Rows 5-17 until piece measures 46³/4", ending by working Row 17, then repeat Row 17 once **more**.

Holding 2 strands together, add additional fringe across short edges of Afghan *(Figs. 28b & d, page 127)*.

# PEEK-A-BOO HEARTS

*A delicate filet crochet pattern gives this endearing afghan an old-fashioned look. Featuring peek-a-boo hearts, the winsome wrap is nice for sharing with a special loved one.*

**Finished Size:** 49" x 61"

## MATERIALS
Worsted Weight Yarn:
  31 ounces, (880 yards, 2,125 grams)
Crochet hook, size H (5.00 mm) **or** size needed for gauge

**GAUGE:** 18 dc and 10 rows = 5¹/4"

*Note:* Each row is worked across length of Afghan.

# BASIC CHART STITCHES
**Beginning Block over Block:** Ch 3 **(counts as first dc)**, turn; dc in next 3 dc.
**Ending Block over Block:** Dc in last 3 dc.
**Block over Block:** Dc in next 3 dc.
**Block over Space:** 2 Dc in next ch-2 sp, dc in next dc.
**Space over Space:** Ch 2, dc in next dc.
**Space over Block:** Ch 2, skip next 2 dc, dc in next dc.

Ch 240 **loosely**.
**Row 1 (Wrong side):** Dc in fourth ch from hook **(3 skipped chs count as first dc)** and in next 2 chs, ★ (ch 2, skip next 2 chs, dc in next ch) 11 times, ch 2, skip next 2 chs, dc in next 4 chs; repeat from ★ across: 94 dc and 72 ch-2 sps.
**Rows 2-91:** Follow Chart Rows 2-11, 9 times; do **not** finish off.
**Edging:** Ch 1, turn; (slip st, ch 2, dc) twice in first dc, skip next 2 dc, [(slip st, ch 2, dc) in next 13 dc, skip next 2 dc] 6 times, (slip st, ch 2, dc, slip st) in last dc, ch 2; working in end of rows, skip first row, (slip st in next row, ch 2); working in free loops of beginning ch *(Fig. 25b, page 126)*, (slip st, ch 2, dc) twice in ch at base of first dc, skip next 2 chs, ★ (slip st, ch 2, dc) in next ch, skip next 2 chs; repeat from ★ across to last ch, (slip st, ch 2, dc, slip st) in last ch, ch 2; working in end of rows, slip st in first row, ch 2, (slip st in next row, ch 2) across to last row, skip last row; join with slip st to first slip st, finish off.

**CHART**

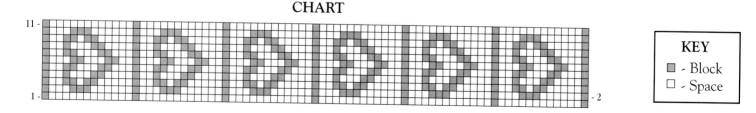

| KEY |
| --- |
| ■ - Block |
| □ - Space |

On right side rows, follow Chart from right to left; on wrong side rows, follow Chart from left to right.

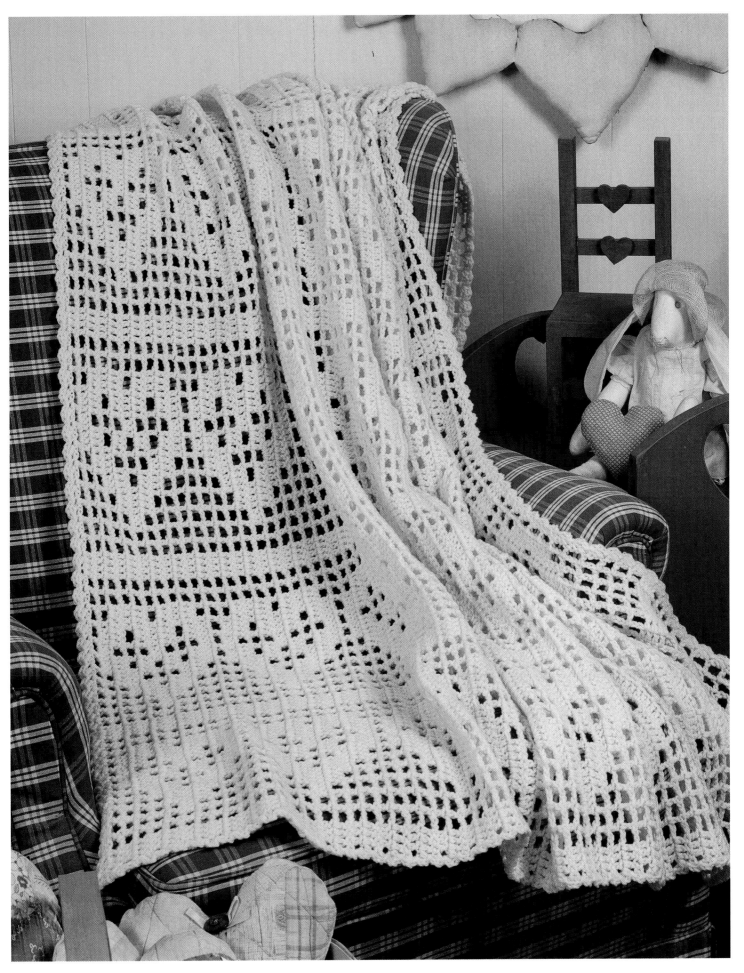

# PATCHWORK HEARTS

*This folksy afghan makes a nifty take-along project because the granny squares are stitched individually and then whipstitched together. The patchwork look is easy to achieve using the convenient placement diagram.*

**Finished Size:** 48" x 69"

## MATERIALS
Worsted Weight Yarn:
Cream - 24 ounces, (680 grams, 1,510 yards)
Rose - 21 ounces, (600 grams, 1,320 yards)
Crochet hook, size I (5.50 mm) **or** size needed for gauge
Yarn needle

**GAUGE:** Each Square = 3"

Referring to the Key, make the number of Squares specified in the colors indicated.

## SQUARE A
With color indicated, ch 4; join with slip st to form a ring.
**Rnd 1 (Right side):** Ch 3 **(counts as first dc, now and throughout)**, 2 dc in ring, ch 2, (3 dc in ring, ch 2) 3 times; join with slip st to first dc: 12 dc and 4 ch-2 sps.
**Note:** Loop a short piece of yarn around any stitch to mark Rnd 1 as **right** side.
**Rnd 2:** Slip st in next 2 dc and in next ch-2 sp, ch 3, (2 dc, ch 2, 3 dc) in same sp, ch 1, ★ (3 dc, ch 2, 3 dc) in next ch-2 sp, ch 1; repeat from ★ 2 times **more**; join with slip st to first dc, finish off: 24 dc and 8 sps.

## SQUARE B
With Cream, ch 4; join with slip st to form a ring.
**Rnd 1 (Right side):** Ch 5 **(counts as first dc plus ch 2)**, 3 dc in ring, cut Cream, with Rose, YO and draw through, ch 1, (3 dc, ch 2, 3 dc) in ring, cut Rose, with Cream, YO and draw through, ch 1, 2 dc in ring; join with slip st to first dc: 12 dc and 4 ch-2 sps.
**Note:** Mark Rnd 1 as **right** side.
**Rnd 2:** Slip st in first ch-2 sp, ch 3, (2 dc, ch 2, 3 dc) in same sp, ch 1, 3 dc in next ch-2 sp, cut Cream, with Rose, YO and draw through, ch 1, 3 dc in same sp, ch 1, (3 dc, ch 2, 3 dc) in next ch-2 sp, ch 1, 3 dc in next ch-2 sp, cut Rose, with Cream, YO and draw through, ch 1, 3 dc in same sp, ch 1; join with slip st to first dc, finish off: 24 dc and 8 sps.

## ASSEMBLY
With matching color, using Placement Diagram as a guide, and working through inside loops only, whipstitch Squares together **(Fig. 26a, page 127)**, forming 15 vertical strips of

22 Squares each, beginning in second ch of first corner ch-2 and ending in first ch of next corner ch-2; whipstitch strips together in same manner.

## EDGING
**Rnd 1:** With **right** side facing, join Cream with sc in any corner ch-2 sp **(see Joining With Sc, page 126)**; sc in same sp, sc evenly around entire Afghan working 3 sc in each corner ch-2 sp, sc in same sp as first sc; join with slip st to first sc.
**Rnd 2:** Ch 1, 2 sc in same st, sc in each sc across to center sc of next corner 3-sc group, ★ 3 sc in center sc, sc in each sc across to center sc of next corner 3-sc group; repeat from ★ 2 times **more**, sc in same st as first sc; join with slip st to first sc, finish off.
**Rnd 3:** With **right** side facing, join Rose with sc in same st as joining; sc in same st and in each sc across to center sc of next corner 3-sc group, ★ 3 sc in center sc, sc in each sc across to center sc of next corner 3-sc group; repeat from ★ 2 times **more**, sc in same st as first sc; join with slip st to first sc.
**Rnd 4:** Ch 1, 2 sc in same st, sc in each sc across to center sc of next corner 3-sc group, ★ 3 sc in center sc, sc in each sc across to center sc of next corner 3-sc group; repeat from ★ 2 times **more**, sc in same st as first sc; join with slip st to first sc, finish off.
**Rnds 5 and 6:** With Cream, repeat Rnds 3 and 4.

### PLACEMENT DIAGRAM

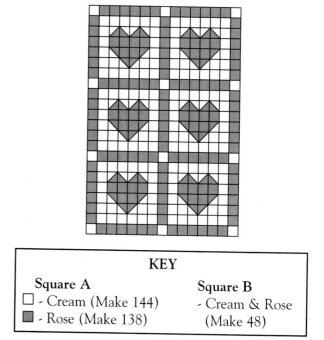

| KEY | |
|---|---|
| **Square A** | **Square B** |
| ☐ - Cream (Make 144) | - Cream & Rose |
| ▨ - Rose (Make 138) | (Make 48) |

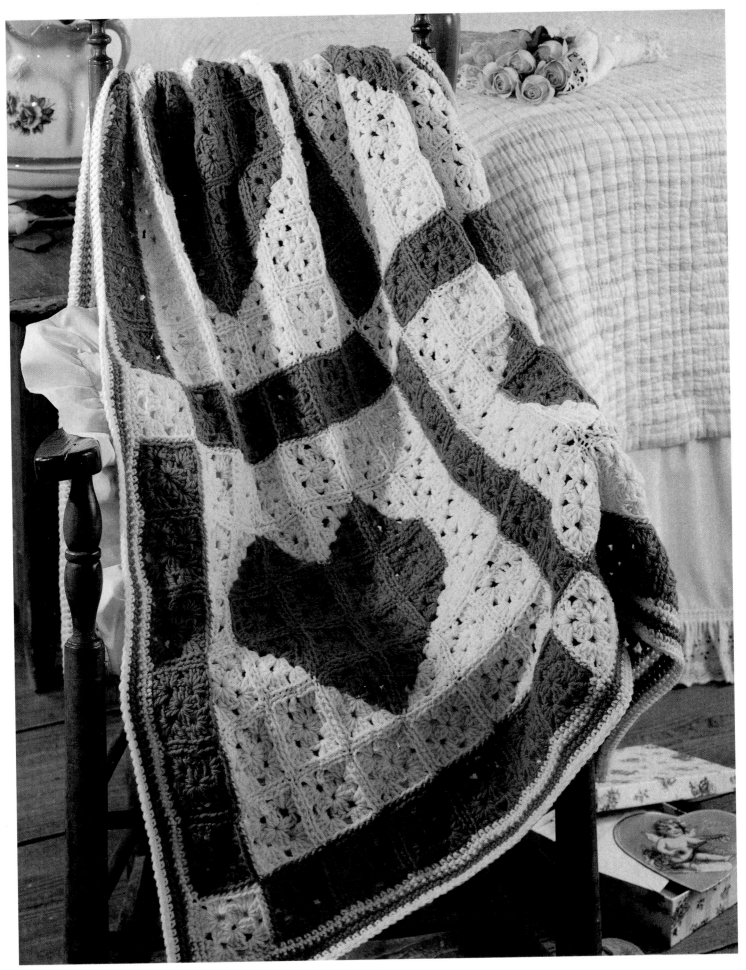

# SWEETHEART BABY WRAP

*A precious gift for a baby girl, this blissful wrap features openwork hearts outlined with soft crocheted ruffles. To create a boy's keepsake afghan, simply substitute blue yarn wherever pink is used.*

**Finished Size:** 38" x 50"

## MATERIALS

Worsted Weight Yarn:
    White - 26 ounces, (740 grams, 1,520 yards)
    Pink - 8 ounces, (230 grams, 470 yards)
Crochet hook, size I (5.50 mm) **or** size needed for gauge
Yarn needle

**GAUGE:** 13 hdc and 11 rows = 4"

With White, ch 118 **loosely**.
**Row 1 (Right side):** Hdc in third ch from hook and in each ch across **(2 skipped chs count as first hdc):** 117 hdc.
*Note:* Loop a short piece of yarn around any stitch to mark Row 1 as **right** side.
**Row 2:** Ch 2 **(counts as first hdc, now and throughout),** turn; hdc in next hdc, ch 1, (skip next hdc, hdc in next hdc, ch 1) across to last 3 hdc, skip next hdc, hdc in last 2 hdc: 57 ch-1 sps.
**Row 3:** Ch 2, turn; hdc in next hdc and in each hdc and each ch-1 sp across: 117 hdc.
**Rows 4-129:** Follow Chart Rows 4-23, 6 times; then follow Rows 4-9 once **more.**

**Row 130:** Ch 2, turn; hdc in next hdc, ch 1, (skip next hdc, hdc in next hdc, ch 1) across to last 3 hdc, skip next hdc, hdc in last 2 hdc: 57 ch-1 sps.
**Row 131:** Ch 2, turn; hdc in next hdc and in each hdc and each ch-1 sp across; finish off: 117 hdc.
**RUFFLE**
With **right** side facing, holding Row 1 away from you, and referring to Chart for placement, join Pink with slip st around post of hdc at Point X of any Heart **(Fig. 10, page 122)**; ch 1, sc in same st, ch 3, 5 dc in side of sc just made, ch 3, (sc around post of hdc at next point, ch 3, 4 dc in side of sc just made, ch 2) 8 times, sc around post of hdc at Point Y, (ch 2, sc around post of hdc at next point, ch 3, 4 dc in side of sc just made) 8 times, ch 3; join with slip st to top of beginning ch-3, finish off.
Repeat around remaining 17 Hearts.

## EDGING

**Rnd 1:** With **right** side facing, join Pink with slip st in first hdc on last row; ch 1, 3 sc in same st, work 111 sc evenly spaced across to last hdc, 3 sc in last hdc; work 129 sc evenly spaced across end of rows to beginning ch; working in free loops of beginning ch **(Fig. 25b, page 126)**, 3 sc in first ch, work 111 sc evenly spaced across to last ch, 3 sc in last ch; work 129 sc evenly spaced across end of rows; join with slip st to first sc: 492 sc.

## CHART

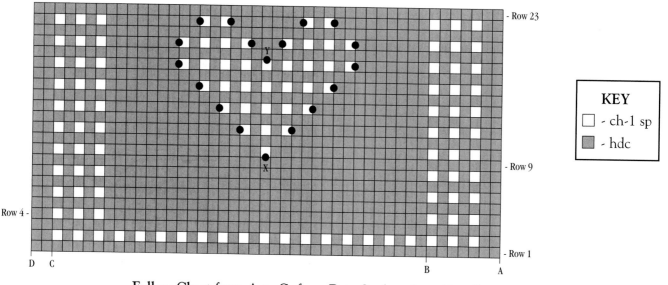

Follow Chart from A to C, from B to C, then from B to D.

**Rnd 2:** Ch 1, sc in same st and in each sc around, working 3 sc in each corner sc; join with slip st to first sc, finish off: 500 sc.

**Rnd 3:** With **right** side facing, join White with slip st in any corner sc; ch 3, 4 dc in same st, sc in next sc, (skip next 2 sc, 5 dc in next sc, skip next 2 sc, sc in next sc) across to next corner sc, ★ 5 dc in corner sc, sc in next sc, (skip next 2 sc, 5 dc in next sc, skip next 2 sc, sc in next sc) across to next corner sc; repeat from ★ around; join with slip st to top of beginning ch-3, finish off.

**Rnd 4:** With **right** side facing, join Pink with slip st in any corner dc; ch 1, sc in same st, 5 dc in next dc, skip next dc, dc in next sc, (skip next 2 dc, 5 dc in next dc, skip next 2 dc, dc in next sc) across to within 2 dc of next corner, skip next dc, 5 dc in next dc, ★ sc in next dc, 5 dc in next dc, skip next dc, dc in next sc, (skip next 2 dc, 5 dc in next dc, skip next 2 dc, dc in next sc) across to within 2 dc of next corner, skip next dc, 5 dc in next dc; repeat from ★ around; join with slip st to first sc, finish off.

Using photo as a guide, weave four strands of Pink through center sp of each group of 3 ch-1 sps.

# COUNTRY AT HEART

*Worked in a classic combination of blue and ecru, this cozy blanket has country appeal! Each block has a stylish border that's echoed in the edging.*

**Finished Size:** 52" x 68"

## MATERIALS
Worsted Weight Yarn:
Ecru - 34$\frac{1}{2}$ ounces, (980 grams, 2,365 yards)
Blue - 22$\frac{1}{2}$ ounces, (640 grams, 1,545 yards)
Crochet hook, size I (5.50 mm) **or** size needed for gauge
Yarn needle

**GAUGE:** Each Square = 8"

**Gauge Swatch:** 5$\frac{1}{4}$"
Work same as Center.
Finish off.

## SQUARE (Make 48)
### CENTER
With Ecru, ch 18 **loosely**.
**Row 1 (Right side):** Sc in third ch from hook **(2 skipped chs count as first hdc)**, (dc in next ch, sc in next ch) across to last ch, hdc in last ch: 17 sts.
*Note:* Loop a short piece of yarn around any stitch to mark Row 1 as **right** side and bottom edge.
**Row 2:** Ch 1, turn; sc in first hdc, (dc in next sc, sc in next st) across.
*Note:* Do **not** carry yarn across back of work. Use a separate ball of yarn for each color change. Cut old yarn when color is no longer needed.
**Row 3:** Ch 2 **(counts as first hdc, now and throughout)**, turn; sc in next dc, (dc in next sc, sc in next dc) 3 times changing to Blue in last sc made **(Fig. 23a, page 126)**, dc in next sc changing to Ecru, sc in next dc, (dc in next sc, sc in next dc) 3 times, hdc in last sc.
*Note:* Continue to change color in same manner.
**Row 4:** Ch 1, turn; sc in first hdc, (dc in next sc, sc in next dc) 3 times, with Blue dc in next sc, sc in next dc, dc in next sc, with Ecru dc in next sc, (dc in next sc, sc in next st) 3 times.
**Row 5:** Ch 2, turn; sc in next dc, (dc in next sc, sc in next dc) twice, with Blue dc in next sc, (sc in next dc, dc in next sc) twice, with Ecru sc in next dc, (dc in next sc, sc in next dc) twice, hdc in last sc.
**Row 6:** Ch 1, turn; sc in first hdc, (dc in next sc, sc in next dc) twice, with Blue dc in next sc, (sc in next dc, dc in next sc) 3 times, with Ecru sc in next dc, (dc in next sc, sc in next st) twice.

**Row 7:** Ch 2, turn; sc in next dc, dc in next sc, sc in next dc, with Blue dc in next sc, (sc in next dc, dc in next sc) 4 times, with Ecru sc in next dc, dc in next sc, sc in next dc, hdc in last sc.
**Row 8:** Ch 1, turn; sc in first hdc, dc in next sc, sc in next dc, with Blue dc in next sc, (sc in next dc, dc in next sc) 5 times, with Ecru sc in next dc, dc in next sc, sc in last hdc.
**Row 9:** Ch 2, turn; sc in next dc, with Blue dc in next sc, (sc in next dc, dc in next sc) 6 times, with Ecru sc in next dc, hdc in last sc.
**Row 10:** Ch 1, turn; sc in first hdc, dc in next sc, with Blue sc in next dc, (dc in next sc, sc in next dc) 6 times, with Ecru dc in next sc, sc in last hdc.
**Row 11:** Ch 2, turn; sc in next dc, with Blue dc in next sc, (sc in next dc, dc in next sc) 6 times, with Ecru sc in next dc, hdc in last sc.
**Row 12:** Ch 1, turn; sc in first hdc, dc in next sc, sc in next dc, with Blue dc in next sc, (sc in next dc, dc in next sc) twice, with Ecru sc in next dc, with Blue dc in next sc, (sc in next dc, dc in next sc) twice, with Ecru sc in next dc, dc in next sc, sc in last hdc.
**Row 13:** Ch 2, turn; sc in next dc, dc in next sc, sc in next dc, ★ with Blue dc in next sc, sc in next dc, dc in next sc, with Ecru sc in next dc, dc in next sc, sc in next dc; repeat from ★ once **more**, hdc in last sc.
**Row 14:** Ch 1, turn; sc in first hdc, (dc in next sc, sc in next st) across.
**Row 15:** Ch 2, turn; sc in next dc, (dc in next sc, sc in next dc) across to last sc, hdc in last sc; do **not** finish off.

## BORDER
**Rnd 1:** Ch 1, do **not** turn; sc in last hdc on Row 15, † ch 1; working across end of rows, skip first row, (sc in next row, ch 1, skip next row) across †; working in free loops of beginning ch **(Fig. 25b, page 126)**, (sc, ch 2, sc) in first ch, ch 1, skip next ch, (sc in next ch, ch 1, skip next ch) 7 times, (sc, ch 2, sc) in next ch, repeat from † to † once; working across sts on Row 15, (sc, ch 2, sc) in first hdc, ch 1, skip next sc, (sc in next dc, ch 1, skip next sc) across, sc in same st as first sc, ch 2; join with slip st to first sc: 36 sc and 36 sps.
**Rnd 2:** Ch 1, **turn;** sc in same st, ch 3, sc in next sc, ★ (ch 1, sc in next sc) 8 times, ch 3, sc in next sc; repeat from ★ 2 times **more**, ch 1, (sc in next sc, ch 1) across; join with slip st to first sc, finish off.

Continued on page 49.

# BABY'S PRETTY PILLOWGHAN

*This cuddly afghan becomes a pretty pillow for the nursery when it's not being used to snuggle baby! The cover-up is simply folded into a pocket that you create with two overlapped blocks.*

**Finished Size:** 37" x 49"

## MATERIALS
Worsted Weight Yarn:
White - 23¹/2 ounces, (670 grams, 1,490 yards)
Pink - 10 ounces, (280 grams, 635 yards)
Green - 4 ounces, (110 grams, 255 yards)
Crochet hook, size F (3.75 mm) **or** size needed for gauge

**GAUGE:** 7 sc and 7 rows = 2"
Each Square = 12¹/4"

## PILLOW SQUARE (Make 2)
### CENTER
With White, ch 20 **loosely**.
**Row 1 (Right side):** Sc in second ch from hook and in each ch across: 19 sc.
*Note:* Loop a short piece of yarn around any stitch to mark Row 1 as **right** side and bottom edge.
**Row 2:** Ch 1, turn; sc in each sc across.
*Note:* When working over unused color, hold it with normal tension and keep yarn to **wrong** side.
**Row 3:** Ch 1, turn; sc in first 9 sc changing to Pink in last sc made **(Fig. 23a, page 126)**, sc in next sc changing to White, sc in last 9 sc.
*Note:* Continue to change colors in same manner.
**Row 4:** Ch 1, turn; sc in first 8 sc, with Pink sc in next 3 sc, with White sc in last 8 sc.
**Row 5:** Ch 1, turn; sc in first 7 sc, with Pink sc in next 5 sc, with White sc in last 7 sc.
**Row 6:** Ch 1, turn; sc in first 6 sc, with Pink sc in next 7 sc, with White sc in last 6 sc.
**Row 7:** Ch 1, turn; sc in first 5 sc, with Pink sc in next 9 sc, with White sc in last 5 sc.
**Row 8:** Ch 1, turn; sc in first 4 sc, with Pink sc in next 11 sc, with White sc in last 4 sc.
**Row 9:** Ch 1, turn; sc in first 3 sc, with Pink sc in next 13 sc, with White sc in last 3 sc.
**Rows 10-14:** Ch 1, turn; sc in first 2 sc, with Pink sc in next 15 sc, with White sc in last 2 sc.
**Row 15:** Ch 1, turn; sc in first 3 sc, with Pink sc in next 13 sc, with White sc in last 3 sc.
**Row 16:** Ch 1, turn; sc in first 4 sc, with Pink sc in next 5 sc, with White sc in next sc, with Pink sc in next 5 sc, with White sc in last 4 sc.

**Row 17:** Ch 1, turn; sc in first 5 sc, with Pink sc in next 3 sc, with White sc in next 3 sc, with Pink sc in next 3 sc, cut Pink; with White sc in last 5 sc.
**Rows 18 and 19:** Ch 1, turn; sc in each sc across. Finish off.

## BORDER
**Rnd 1:** With **right** side facing, join Pink with sc in first sc on Row 19 **(see Joining With Sc, page 126)**; 2 sc in same st, sc in each sc across to last sc, 3 sc in last sc; work 17 sc evenly spaced across end of rows; working in free loops of beginning ch **(Fig. 25b, page 126)**, 3 sc in first ch, sc in next 17 chs, 3 sc in next ch; work 17 sc evenly spaced across end of rows; join with slip st to first sc, finish off: 80 sc.
**Rnd 2:** With **right** side facing, join White with sc in center sc of any corner 3-sc group; ch 2, sc in same st, ch 2, skip next sc, (sc in next sc, ch 2, skip next sc) across to center sc of next corner 3-sc group, ★ (sc, ch 2) twice in center sc, skip next sc, (sc in next sc, ch 2, skip next sc) across to center sc of next corner 3-sc group; repeat from ★ 2 times **more**; join with slip st to first sc: 44 ch-2 sps.
**Rnd 3:** Slip st in first ch-2 sp, ch 1, (sc, ch 2, sc) in same sp, ch 3, (sc in next ch-2 sp, ch 3) across to next corner ch-2 sp, ★ (sc, ch 2, sc) in corner ch-2 sp, ch 3, (sc in next ch-2 sp, ch 3) across to next corner ch-2 sp; repeat from ★ 2 times **more**; join with slip st to first sc, finish off: 48 sps.
**Rnd 4:** With **right** side facing, join Green with slip st in any corner ch-2 sp; ch 3 **(counts as first dc, now and throughout)**, (2 dc, ch 2, 3 dc) in same sp, ch 1, skip next ch-3 sp, (3 dc in next ch-3 sp, ch 1, skip next ch-3 sp) across to next corner ch-2 sp, ★ (3 dc, ch 2, 3 dc) in corner ch-2 sp, ch 1, skip next ch-3 sp, (3 dc in next ch-3 sp, ch 1, skip next ch-3 sp) across to next corner ch-2 sp; repeat from ★ 2 times **more**; join with slip st to first dc, finish off: 84 dc.
**Rnd 5:** With **right** side facing, join White with sc in any corner ch-2 sp; ch 2, sc in same sp, ch 2, skip next dc, sc in next dc, ch 2, (sc in next ch-1 sp, ch 2, skip next dc, sc in next dc, ch 2) across to next corner ch-2 sp, ★ (sc, ch 2) twice in corner ch-2 sp, skip next dc, sc in next dc, ch 2, (sc in next ch-1 sp, ch 2, skip next dc, sc in next dc, ch 2) across to next corner ch-2 sp; repeat from ★ 2 times **more**; join with slip st to first sc: 60 ch-2 sps.

Continued on page 48.

**Rnd 6:** Slip st in first ch-2 sp, ch 1, (sc in same sp, ch 3) twice, (sc in next ch-2 sp, ch 3) across to next corner ch-2 sp, ★ (sc, ch 3) twice in corner ch-2 sp, (sc in next ch-2 sp, ch 3) across to next corner ch-2 sp; repeat from ★ 2 times **more**; join with slip st to first sc, finish off: 64 ch-3 sps.

**Rnd 7:** With **right** side facing, join Pink with slip st in any corner ch-3 sp; ch 3, (2 dc, ch 2, 3 dc) in same sp, ch 1, skip next ch-3 sp, (3 dc in next ch-3 sp, ch 1, skip next ch-3 sp) across to next corner ch-3 sp, ★ (3 dc, ch 2, 3 dc) in corner ch-3 sp, ch 1, skip next ch-3 sp, (3 dc in next ch-3 sp, ch 1, skip next ch-3 sp) across to next corner ch-3 sp; repeat from ★ 2 times **more**; join with slip st to first dc, finish off: 108 dc.

**Rnd 8:** With **right** side facing, join White with sc in top right corner ch-2 sp; ch 2, sc in same sp, ch 2, skip next dc, sc in next dc, ch 2, (sc in next ch-1 sp, ch 2, skip next dc, sc in next dc, ch 2) across to next corner ch-2 sp, ★ (sc, ch 2) twice in corner ch-2 sp, skip next dc, sc in next dc, ch 2, (sc in next ch-1 sp, ch 2, skip next dc, sc in next dc, ch 2) across to next corner ch-2 sp; repeat from ★ 2 times **more**; join with slip st to first sc: 76 ch-2 sps.

**Rnd 9:** Slip st in first ch-2 sp, ch 1, (sc in same sp, ch 3) twice, (sc in next ch-2 sp, ch 3) across to next corner ch-2 sp, ★ (sc, ch 3) twice in corner ch-2 sp, (sc in next ch-2 sp, ch 3) across to next corner ch-2 sp; repeat from ★ 2 times **more**; join with slip st to first sc, finish off: 80 ch-3 sps.

## ASSEMBLY

To assemble, place one Pillow Square on top of the other with **right** side of each facing up; pin to hold layers together. When joining Squares 1 and 2 to the Pillow Squares, work through **both** Pillow Squares; when joining Square 4 to the Pillow Square, **work through top Pillow Square only**, leaving the **top** edge of bottom Pillow Square unjoined to be used for pocket (**Fig. 1**).

Fig. 1

| 9 | 10 | 11 |
|---|---|---|
| 6 | 7 | 8 |
| 3 | 4 | 5 |
| 1<br>Join → | Pillow<br>Squares<br>Join<br>↓ | 2<br>← Join |

## REMAINING 11 SQUARES

Work same as Pillow Square through Rnd 7: 108 dc.

**Rnd 8:** Referring to *Fig. 1* for the order in which to join the Squares, join yarn as follows: For Square 1, join in top right corner; for Square 2, join in bottom left corner; for all remaining Squares, join in bottom right corner; continue same as Rnd 8 of Pillow Square: 76 ch-2 sps.

**Rnd 9 (Joining rnd):** Work One or Two Side Joining, arranging Squares around Pillow Squares.

## ONE SIDE JOINING

**Rnd 9 (Joining rnd):** Slip st in first ch-2 sp, ch 1, sc in same sp, ch 3, (sc in next ch-2 sp, ch 3) across to next corner ch-2 sp, ★ (sc, ch 3) twice in corner ch-2 sp, (sc in next ch-2 sp, ch 3) across to next corner ch-2 sp; repeat from ★ once **more**, sc in corner ch-2 sp, ch 1, holding Squares with **wrong** sides together, sc in corresponding corner ch-3 sp on **adjacent** Square (*Fig. 21, page 124*), ch 1, sc in same sp on **new** Square, ch 1, sc in next ch-3 sp on **adjacent** Square, ch 1, (sc in next ch-2 sp on **new** Square, ch 1, sc in next ch-3 sp on **adjacent** Square, ch 1) across to next corner ch-2 sp on **new** Square, sc in same corner ch-2 sp as first sc, ch 1, sc in corner ch-3 sp on **adjacent** Square, ch 1; join with slip st to first sc on **new** Square, finish off.

## TWO SIDE JOINING

**Rnd 9 (Joining rnd):** Slip st in first ch-2 sp, ch 1, sc in same sp, ch 3, (sc in next ch-2 sp, ch 3) across to next corner ch-2 sp, (sc, ch 3) twice in corner ch-2 sp, (sc in next ch-2 sp, ch 3) across to next corner ch-2 sp, sc in corner ch-2 sp, ch 1, holding Squares with **wrong** sides together, sc in corresponding corner ch-3 sp on **adjacent** Square, ch 1, sc in same sp on **new** Square, † ch 1, sc in next ch-3 sp on **adjacent** Square, ch 1, (sc in next ch-2 sp on **new** Square, ch 1, sc in next ch-3 sp on **adjacent** Square, ch 1) across to next corner ch-2 sp on **new** Square †, sc in corner ch-2 sp, ch 1, sc in **each** of next 3 corner sps on **adjacent** Squares, ch 1, sc in same sp on **new** Square; repeat from † to † once, sc in same corner ch-2 sp as first sc, ch 1, sc in corner ch-3 sp on **adjacent** Square, ch 1; join with slip st to first sc on **new** Square, finish off.

## EDGING

With **right** side facing and working through **both** Pillow Squares along bottom edge, join White with sc in any corner ch-3 sp; ch 3, sc in same sp, ch 3, (sc in next ch-sp, ch 3) across to next corner ch-3 sp, ★ (sc, ch 3) twice in corner ch-3 sp, (sc in next ch-sp, ch 3) across to next corner ch-3 sp; repeat from ★ 2 times **more**; join with slip st to first sc, finish off.

# FOLDING

Spread Afghan with **right** side facing. Fold two outside Strips **over** center Strip, then fold in quarters **over** pocket. Turn the pocket **over** folded Afghan to form pillow (**Fig. 2**).

**Fig. 2**

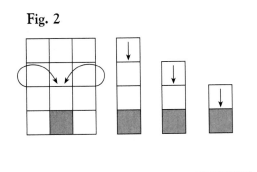

# COUNTRY AT HEART

Continued from page 44.

**Rnd 3:** With **right** side facing, join Blue with sc in first sc to right of any corner ch-3 (*see Joining With Sc, page 126*); working **behind** next corner ch-3, (dc, ch 3, dc) in ch-2 sp one rnd **below**, ★ sc in next sc, (working **behind** next ch-1, dc in ch-1 sp one rnd **below**, sc in next sc) 8 times, working **behind** next corner ch-3, (dc, ch 3, dc) in ch-2 sp one rnd **below**; repeat from ★ 2 times **more**, (sc in next sc, working **behind** next ch-1, dc in ch-1 sp one rnd **below**) across; join with slip st to first sc: 76 sts and 4 ch-3 sps.

**Rnd 4:** Ch 1, **turn**; sc in same st, ch 1, skip next dc, ★ (sc in next sc, ch 1, skip next dc) across to next corner ch-3 sp, (sc, ch 3, sc) in corner ch-3 sp, ch 1, skip next dc; repeat from ★ around; join with slip st to first sc, finish off: 44 sc and 44 sps.

**Rnd 5:** With **right** side facing, join Ecru with sc in first sc to right of any corner ch-3; working **behind** next corner ch-3, (dc, ch 3, dc) in ch-3 sp one rnd **below**, ★ sc in next sc, (working **behind** next ch-1, dc in dc one rnd **below**, sc in next sc) across to next corner ch-3, working **behind** corner ch-3, (dc, ch 3, dc) in ch-3 sp one rnd **below**; repeat from ★ 2 times **more**, (sc in next sc, working **behind** next ch-1, dc in dc one rnd **below**) across; join with slip st to first sc, finish off: 92 sts and 4 ch-3 sps.

# ASSEMBLY

Using Ecru, matching sts of bottom edge of one Square to top edge of next Square, and working through both loops, whipstitch Squares together (*Fig. 26b, page 127*), forming 6 vertical strips of 8 Squares each, beginning in center ch of first corner ch-3 and ending in center ch of next corner ch-3; whipstitch strips together in same manner, keeping bottom edges at same end and always working in same direction.

# EDGING

**Rnd 1:** With **right** side facing, join Ecru with sc in any corner ch-3 sp; ch 2, sc in same sp, ★ † sc in next 23 sts, (sc in next sp, hdc in joining, sc in next sp and in next 23 sts) across to next corner ch-3 sp †, (sc, ch 2, sc) in corner ch-3 sp; repeat from ★ 2 times **more**, then repeat from † to † once; join with slip st to first sc: 724 sts and 4 ch-2 sps.

**Rnd 2:** Ch 1, **turn**; sc in same st, (ch 1, skip next st, sc in next sc) across to next corner ch-2, ch 3, skip corner ch-2, ★ sc in next sc, (ch 1, skip next st, sc in next sc) across to next corner ch-2, ch 3, skip corner ch-2; repeat from ★ 2 times **more**; join with slip st to first sc, finish off: 364 sc and 4 ch-3 sps.

**Rnd 3:** With **right** side facing, join Blue with sc in first sc to right of any corner ch-3; working **behind** next corner ch-3, (dc, ch 3, dc) in ch-2 sp one rnd **below**, ★ sc in next sc, (working **behind** next ch-1, dc in st one rnd **below**, sc in next sc) across to next corner ch-3, working **behind** corner ch-3, (dc, ch 3, dc) in ch-2 sp one rnd **below**; repeat from ★ 2 times **more**, (sc in next sc, working **behind** next ch-1, dc in st one rnd **below**) across; join with slip st to first sc: 732 sts and 4 ch-3 sps.

**Rnd 4:** Ch 1, **turn**; sc in same st, ch 1, skip next dc, ★ (sc in next sc, ch 1, skip next dc) across to next corner ch-3 sp, (sc, ch 3, sc) in corner ch-3 sp, ch 1, skip next dc; repeat from ★ around; join with slip st to first sc, finish off: 372 sts and 4 ch-3 sps.

**Rnd 5:** With **right** side facing, join Ecru with sc in first sc to right of any corner ch-3; working **behind** next corner ch-3, (dc, ch 3, dc) in ch-3 sp one rnd **below**, ★ sc in next sc, (working **behind** next ch-1, dc in dc one rnd **below**, sc in next sc) across to next corner ch-3, working **behind** corner ch-3, (dc, ch 3, dc) in ch-3 sp one rnd **below**; repeat from ★ 2 times **more**, (sc in next sc, working **behind** next ch-1, dc in dc one rnd **below**) across; join with slip st to first sc: 748 sts and 4 ch-3 sps.

**Rnd 6:** Ch 2, do **not** turn; skip next dc, (slip st, ch 3, slip st) in next corner ch-3 sp, ★ ch 2, skip next dc, (slip st in next sc, ch 2, skip next dc) across to next corner ch-3 sp, (slip st, ch 3, slip st) in corner ch-3 sp; repeat from ★ 2 times **more**, ch 2, skip next dc, (slip st in next sc, ch 2, skip next dc) across; join with slip st to base of beginning ch-2, finish off.

# HOME
## fires burn brightest

*Crackling wood, spritely dancing flames, and the warm glow of embers — the soothing sights and sounds of the hearth are what make curling up by the fire so pleasant! Now you can enjoy your fireside retreat even more with some of the coziest cover-ups ever. In this special collection, you'll discover rustic wraps as well as afghans tailored for formal settings. Like a comforting old friend, any of these handmade throws will offer a relaxing way to enjoy the long days of winter.*

# GLOWING EMBERS

*Worked in warm hues, this delightful cover-up is reminiscent of a bed
of glowing embers. Long double crochets create the eye-pleasing pattern.*

**Finished Size:** 50" x 68"

## MATERIALS

Worsted Weight Yarn:
Black - 34$\frac{1}{2}$ ounces, (980 grams, 2,365 yards)
Gold - 18$\frac{1}{2}$ ounces, (530 grams, 1,270 yards)
Dk Red - 17 ounces, (480 grams, 1,165 yards)
Crochet hook, size G (4.00 mm) **or** size needed for gauge

**GAUGE:** In pattern, 17 sts and 16 rows = 4"

**Gauge Swatch:** 4$\frac{1}{4}$"w x 4"h
Ch 21 **loosely.**
Work same as Afghan for 16 rows.
Finish off.

## STITCH GUIDE

**LONG DOUBLE CROCHET** *(abbreviated LDC)*
YO, working **around** ch-2 on previous 2 rows, insert
hook in next sc 3 rows **below,** YO and pull up a loop
even with hook *(Fig. 17, page 123)*, (YO and draw
through 2 loops on hook) twice.

With Black, ch 211 **loosely.**
**Row 1 (Wrong side):** Sc in second ch from hook and in
each ch across; finish off: 210 sc.
**Note:** Loop a short piece of yarn around the **back** of any
stitch on Row 1 to mark **right** side.
**Row 2:** With **right** side facing, join Gold with slip st in
first sc; ch 1, sc in next sc, hdc in next sc, dc in next 4 sc,
hdc in next sc, sc in next sc, ★ ch 2, skip next 2 sc, sc in
next sc, hdc in next sc, dc in next 4 sc, hdc in next sc,
sc in next sc; repeat from ★ across to last sc, slip st in
last sc: 170 sts and 20 ch-2 sps.

**Row 3:** Ch 1, turn; skip first slip st, sc in next sc, hdc in
next hdc, dc in next 4 dc, hdc in next hdc, sc in next sc,
★ ch 2, sc in next sc, hdc in next hdc, dc in next 4 dc,
hdc in next hdc, sc in next sc; repeat from ★ across to
last ch, slip st in last ch; finish off.
**Row 4:** With **right** side facing, join Black with sc in first
slip st *(see Joining With Sc, page 126)*; sc in next 8 sts,
(work 2 LDC, sc in next 8 sts) across to turning ch, sc in
turning ch: 210 sts.
**Row 5:** Ch 1, turn; sc in each st across; finish off.
**Row 6:** With **right** side facing, join Dk Red with slip st in
first sc; ch 3 **(counts as first dc, now and throughout),**
dc in next sc, hdc in next sc, sc in next sc, ch 2, skip next
2 sc, sc in next sc, hdc in next sc, ★ dc in next 4 sc, hdc in
next sc, sc in next sc, ch 2, skip next 2 sc, sc in next sc,
hdc in next sc; repeat from ★ across to last 2 sc, dc in last
2 sc: 168 sts and 21 ch-2 sps.
**Row 7:** Ch 3, turn; dc in next dc, hdc in next hdc, sc in
next sc, ch 2, sc in next sc, hdc in next hdc, ★ dc in next
4 dc, hdc in next hdc, sc in next sc, ch 2, sc in next sc,
hdc in next hdc; repeat from ★ across to last 2 dc, dc in
last 2 dc; finish off.
**Row 8:** With **right** side facing, join Black with sc in first
dc; sc in next 3 sts, work 2 LDC, (sc in next 8 sts, work
2 LDC) across to last 4 sts, sc in last 4 sts: 210 sts.
**Row 9:** Ch 1, turn; sc in each st across; finish off.
**Rows 10-268:** Repeat Rows 2-9, 32 times; then repeat
Rows 2-4 once **more.**
Do **not** finish off.

## EDGING

**Rnds 1 and 2:** Ch 1, do **not** turn; sc evenly around
working 3 sc in each corner; join with slip st to first sc.
Finish off.

Holding 6 strands of Black together, add fringe evenly
across short edges of Afghan *(Figs. 28a & c, page 127)*.

53

# CRISSCROSS COVER-UP

*Rows of crisscrossing treble crochets add rich texture to this snuggly wrap made with brushed acrylic yarn. The brilliant strips are whipstitched together for a quick finish.*

**Finished Size:** 46" x 65"

## MATERIALS
Worsted Weight Brushed Acrylic Yarn:
Red - 38 ounces, (1,080 grams, 2,930 yards)
Green - 6 ounces, (170 grams, 465 yards)
Crochet hook, size G (4.00 mm) **or** size needed for gauge
Yarn needle

**GAUGE:** Each Strip = 3¼" wide

**Gauge Swatch:** 3¼"w x 7¾"h
Ch 23 **loosely.**
Work same as Center.
Work Border.

## STITCH GUIDE

> **DOUBLE TREBLE CROCHET (abbreviated dtr)**
> YO 3 times, insert hook in sp indicated, YO and pull up a loop, (YO and draw through 2 loops on hook) 4 times *(Figs. 8a & b, page 121)*.

# STRIP (Make 14)
## CENTER
With Red, ch 253 **loosely.**
**Row 1:** Sc in second ch from hook and in each ch across: 252 sc.
**Row 2 (Right side):** Ch 1, turn; sc in each sc across.
**Note:** Loop a short piece of yarn around last sc made to mark Row 2 as **right** side and bottom edge.
**Row 3:** Ch 3 **(counts as first dc, now and throughout)**, turn; dc in next sc, ★ skip next 2 sc, tr in next 2 sc, working **behind** tr just made, tr in first skipped sc and in next skipped sc, skip next 2 sc, tr in next 2 sc, working in **front** of tr just made, tr in first skipped sc and in next skipped sc, dc in next 2 sc; repeat from ★ across.
**Row 4:** Ch 3, turn; dc in next dc, ★ skip next 2 tr, tr in next 2 tr, working **behind** tr just made, tr in first skipped tr and in next skipped tr, skip next 2 tr, tr in next 2 tr, working in **front** of tr just made, tr in first skipped tr and in next skipped tr, dc in next 2 dc; repeat from ★ across.
**Row 5:** Ch 1, turn; sc in each st across.
**Row 6:** Ch 1, turn; sc in each sc across, changing to Green in last sc *(Fig. 23a, page 126)*; do **not** finish off.

## BORDER
**Rnd 1:** Ch 1, do **not** turn; 2 sc in last sc on Row 6; † working in end of rows, sc in first row, hdc in next row, (dc, tr, dtr) in next row, (dtr, tr, dc) in next row, hdc in next row, sc in last row †; working in free loops of beginning ch *(Fig. 25b, page 126)*, 2 sc in ch at base of first sc, sc in each ch across to last ch, 2 sc in last ch, repeat from † to † once, 2 sc in first sc on Row 6, sc in each sc across changing to Red in last sc; join with slip st to first sc: 528 sts.
**Rnd 2:** Ch 1, sc in same st and in next sc, † place marker around last sc made for joining placement, sc in same st and in next 4 sts, 2 sc in each of next 2 dtr, sc in next 4 sts, 2 sc in next sc, place marker around last sc made for joining placement †, sc in next 253 sc, repeat from † to † once, sc in each sc across; join with slip st to first sc, finish off.

# ASSEMBLY
Place two Strips with **wrong** sides together and bottom edges at same end. Using Red and working through inside loops only, whipstitch Strips together *(Fig. 26a, page 127)*, beginning in first marked sc and ending in next marked sc.

Join remaining Strips in same manner, always working in same direction.

# HEARTHSIDE RIDGES

*Our classic cover-up reflects country simplicity at its best.*
*The all-natural afghan features raised post-stitch ridges.*

**Finished Size:** 49" x 66"

## MATERIALS
Worsted Weight Yarn:
  Tan - 32 ounces, (910 grams, 2,010 yards)
  Beige - 23 ounces, (650 grams, 1,445 yards)
Crochet hook, size G (4.00 mm) **or** size needed for gauge
Yarn needle

**GAUGE:** Each Strip = 3³/₄" wide

**Gauge Swatch:** 3³/₄"w x 8¹/₂"h
Ch 23 **loosely.**
Work same as Center.
Work Border.

## STITCH GUIDE

> **DOUBLE TREBLE CROCHET** *(abbreviated dtr)*
> YO 3 times, insert hook in sp indicated, YO and pull up a loop, (YO and draw through 2 loops on hook) 4 times *(Figs. 8a & b, page 121).*
> **FRONT POST TREBLE CROCHET**
>   *(abbreviated FPtr)*
> YO twice, insert hook from **front** to **back** around post of st indicated, YO and pull up a loop *(Fig. 12, page 122),* (YO and draw through 2 loops on hook) 3 times. Skip st behind FPtr .
> **FRONT POST HALF DOUBLE CROCHET**
>   *(abbreviated FPhdc)*
> YO, insert hook from **front** to **back** around post of st indicated, YO and pull up a loop *(Fig. 11, page 122),* YO and draw through all 3 loops on hook.

## STRIP (Make 13)
### CENTER
With Beige, ch 267 **loosely.**
**Row 1 (Right side):** Dc in fourth ch from hook (**3 skipped chs count as first dc**) and in next 2 chs, ch 1, (skip next ch, dc in next 3 chs, ch 1) across to last 5 chs, skip next ch, dc in last 4 chs: 200 dc and 65 ch-1 sps.
**Note:** Loop a short piece of yarn around last dc made to mark bottom edge and to mark Row 1 as **right** side.

**Row 2:** Ch 3 (**counts as first dc, now and throughout**), turn; (dc in next 3 dc, ch 1) across to last 4 dc, dc in last 4 dc, changing to Tan in last dc (*Fig. 23a, page 126*); do **not** finish off.

## BORDER
**Rnd 1:** Ch 3, turn; dc in next dc, † work FPtr around next dc, ★ dc in next st, dc in next sp and in next st, work FPtr around next dc; repeat from ★ across to last 2 sts, dc in last 2 sts; working in end of rows, (dc, tr, dtr) in first row, ch 2, (dtr, tr, dc) in last row †; working in free loops of beginning ch (*Fig. 25b, page 126*), dc in first 2 chs, repeat from † to † once; join with slip st to first dc: 542 sts and 2 ch-2 sps.
**Rnd 2:** Ch 3, do **not** turn; working in Back Loops Only (*Fig. 24, page 126*), dc in next dc, † work FPtr around next FPtr, dc in next 3 dc) 66 times, working in sts and in chs, 2 tr in each of next 6 sts †, dc in next 3 dc, repeat from † to † once, dc in last dc changing to Beige; join with slip st to first dc: 558 sts.
**Rnd 3:** Ch 1, working in Back Loops Only, sc in same st and in next dc, † work FPhdc around next FPtr, place marker around FPhdc just made for joining placement, (sc in next 3 dc, work FPhdc around next FPtr) 65 times, place marker around last FPhdc made for joining placement, (sc in next 3 sts, work 2 FPhdc around next tr) twice, 2 sc in each of next 2 tr †, (work 2 FPhdc around next tr, sc in next 3 sts) twice, repeat from † to † once, work 2 FPhdc around next tr, sc in next 3 tr, work 2 FPhdc around next tr, sc in last dc; join with slip st to both loops of first sc, finish off.

## ASSEMBLY
Place two Strips with **wrong** sides together and bottom edges at same end. Using Beige and working through inside loops only, whipstitch Strips together (*Fig. 26a, page 127*), beginning in first marked FPhdc and ending in next marked FPhdc.

Join remaining Strips in same manner, always working in same direction.

# TIMELESS TRACKS

*A timeless addition to the living room, this sophisticated afghan is given dimension with a repeating pattern of post-stitch "railroad tracks." The tailored strips are a breeze to complete.*

**Finished Size:** 45" x 66"

## MATERIALS

Worsted Weight Yarn:
    Red - 30 ounces, (850 grams, 1,885 yards)
    Green - 28 ounces, (800 grams, 1,760 yards)
Crochet hook, size G (4.00 mm) **or** size needed for gauge
Yarn needle

**GAUGE:** 16 dc and 8 rows = 4"
        Each Strip = 2¹/2" wide

## STITCH GUIDE

**FRONT POST TREBLE CROCHET**
*(abbreviated FPtr)*
YO twice, insert hook from **front** to **back** around post of st indicated, YO and pull up a loop *(Fig. 12, page 122)*, (YO and draw through 2 loops on hook) 3 times. Skip st behind FPtr.

## STRIP (Make 18)
### CENTER
With Red, ch 252 **loosely.**
**Row 1 (Right side):** Dc in fourth ch from hook and in each ch across: 250 sts.
**Note:** Loop a short piece of yarn around last dc made to mark bottom edge and to mark Row 1 as **right** side.
**Rows 2 and 3:** Ch 3 **(counts as first dc, now and throughout)**, turn; dc in next dc and in each st across: 250 dc.
Finish off.

## BORDER

**Rnd 1:** With **right** side facing and working in end of rows across bottom edge, join Green with slip st in Row 3; ch 3, 2 dc in same row, 5 tr in Row 2, 3 dc in Row 1; working in free loops of beginning ch *(Fig. 25b, page 126)*, sc in first 4 chs, work FPtr around fifth dc on Row 2, work FPtr around next dc on Row 2, ★ sc in next 3 chs, skip next 3 dc on Row 2, work FPtr around each of next 2 dc; repeat from ★ 47 times **more**, sc in next 4 chs; working in end of rows, 3 dc in Row 1, 5 tr in Row 2, 3 dc in Row 3; working across Row 3, sc in first 4 dc, work FPtr around fifth dc on Row 2 (same dc as FPtr on opposite side), work FPtr around next dc on Row 2, † sc in next 3 dc, skip next 3 dc on Row 2, work FPtr around each of next 2 dc †, repeat from † to † across to last 4 dc, sc in last 4 dc; join with slip st to first dc: 522 sts.
**Rnd 2:** Ch 1, working in Back Loops Only *(Fig. 24, page 126)*, sc in same st and in next 2 dc, † 2 sc in each of next 5 tr, sc in next 4 sts, place marker around last sc made for joining placement, sc in next 249 sts, place marker around last sc made for joining placement †, sc in next 3 dc, repeat from † to † once; join with slip st to both loops of first sc, finish off.

## ASSEMBLY

Place two Strips with **wrong** sides together and bottom edges at the same end. Using Green and working through inside loops only, whipstitch Strips together *(Fig. 26a, page 127)*, beginning in first marked sc and ending in next marked sc.

Join remaining Strips in same manner, always working in same direction.

# RELAXING RIPPLE

*Rows of treble and cluster stitches in progressive colors form the soothing ripples on our mesmerizing afghan. The relaxing waves of blue make this throw a naptime must.*

**Finished Size:** 48" x 64"

## MATERIALS
Worsted Weight Yarn:
Dk Blue - 8 ounces, (230 grams, 595 yards)
Med Blue - 7 ounces, (200 grams, 520 yards)
Blue - 7 ounces, (200 grams, 520 yards)
Lt Blue - 7 ounces, (200 grams, 520 yards)
Crochet hook, size I (5.50 mm) **or** size needed for gauge

**GAUGE:** Each repeat from point to point = 4³/₄"
and 8 rows = 5¹/₄"

**Gauge Swatch:** 9¹/₂"w x 5¹/₄"h
Ch 42 **loosely.**
Work same as Afghan for 8 rows.
Finish off.

## STITCH GUIDE

**CLUSTER** (uses next 3 sts)
YO twice, insert hook in **next** st, YO and pull up a loop, (YO and draw through 2 loops on hook) twice, YO twice, skip **next** st, insert hook in **next** st, YO and pull up a loop, (YO and draw through 2 loops on hook) twice, YO and draw through all 3 loops on hook **(Figs. 16c & d, page 123).**

## COLOR SEQUENCE
2 Rows **each:** Dk Blue **(Fig. 23a, page 126),** ★ Med Blue, Blue, Lt Blue, Dk Blue; repeat from ★ throughout.

With Dk Blue, ch 194 **loosely.**
**Row 1** (Right side)**:** Tr in fifth ch from hook **(4 skipped chs count as first tr),** (ch 1, tr in same ch) twice, skip next ch, (tr in next ch, skip next ch) 3 times, work Cluster, skip next ch, (tr in next ch, skip next ch) 3 times, [(tr, ch 1) twice, 2 tr] in next ch, ★ [2 tr, (ch 1, tr) twice] in next ch, skip next ch, (tr in next ch, skip next ch) 3 times, work Cluster, skip next ch, (tr in next ch, skip next ch) 3 times, [(tr, ch 1) twice, 2 tr] in next ch; repeat from ★ across: 150 sts and 40 ch-1 sps.
**Row 2:** Ch 1, turn; sc in each st and in each ch-1 sp across: 190 sc.
**Row 3:** Ch 4 **(counts as first tr),** turn; tr in same st, (ch 1, tr in same st) twice, skip next sc, (tr in next sc, skip next sc) 3 times, work Cluster, skip next sc, (tr in next sc, skip next sc) 3 times, [(tr, ch 1) twice, 2 tr] in next sc, ★ [2 tr, (ch 1, tr) twice] in next sc, skip next sc, (tr in next sc, skip next sc) 3 times, work Cluster, skip next sc, (tr in next sc, skip next sc) 3 times, [(tr, ch 1) twice, 2 tr] in next sc; repeat from ★ across.
**Row 4:** Ch 1, turn; sc in each st and in each ch-1 sp across.
Repeat Rows 3 and 4 until Afghan measures 64" from beginning ch, ending by working 2 rows Dk Blue.
Finish off.

# COZY CLUSTERS

*A blanket of simple earth-tone clusters, this cozy wrap can be finished
in no time! Coordinating fringe completes the handsome afghan.*

**Finished Size:** 45" x 63"

## MATERIALS
Worsted Weight Yarn:
 Beige - 20¹/₂ ounces, (580 grams, 1,160 yards)
 Tan - 20¹/₂ ounces, (580 grams, 1,160 yards)
 Lt Brown - 20¹/₂ ounces, (580 grams, 1,160 yards)
Crochet hook, size J (6.00 mm) **or** size needed for gauge

**GAUGE:** In pattern, 5 3-dc Clusters = 3¹/₂" and
 8 rows = 3³/₄"

**Gauge Swatch:** 4"w x 3³/₄"h
With Beige, ch 12 **loosely**.
Work same as Afghan for 8 rows.

*Note:* Each row is worked across length of Afghan.
 When joining yarn and finishing off, always leave
 an 8" end to be worked into fringe.

## STITCH GUIDE

**3-DC CLUSTER**
★ YO, insert hook in st or sp indicated, YO and pull up a
loop, YO and draw through 2 loops on hook; repeat from
★ 2 times **more**, YO and draw through all 4 loops on
hook *(Figs. 16a & b, page 123)*.
**2-DC CLUSTER**
★ YO, insert hook in st indicated, YO and pull up a
loop, YO and draw through 2 loops on hook; repeat
from ★ once **more**, YO and draw through all 3 loops
on hook.
**V-ST**
(Hdc, ch 1, hdc) in ch-1 sp indicated.

## COLOR SEQUENCE
One row **each**: Beige, ★ Tan, Lt Brown, Beige; repeat from
★ 31 times **more**.

With Beige, ch 182 **loosely**.
**Row 1** (Right side): Sc in second ch from hook and in
each ch across: 181 sc.
*Note:* Loop a short piece of yarn around any stitch to mark
Row 1 as **right** side.
**Row 2:** With **wrong** side facing, join next color with slip st
in first sc; ch 2, dc in same st, ch 1, ★ skip next sc, work
3-dc Cluster in next sc, ch 1; repeat from ★ across to last
2 sc, skip next sc, work 2-dc Cluster in last sc; finish off:
90 ch-1 sps.
**Row 3:** With **right** side facing, join next color with slip st
in first 2-dc Cluster; ch 2, work V-St in next ch-1 sp and in
each ch-1 sp across to last dc, hdc in last dc; finish off:
90 V-Sts.
**Row 4:** With **wrong** side facing, join next color with
slip st in first hdc; ch 3 **(counts as first dc)**, work
3-dc Cluster in next ch-1 sp, (ch 1, work 3-dc Cluster in
next ch-1 sp) across to last hdc, skip last hdc, dc in next
ch; finish off: 89 ch-1 sps.
**Row 5:** With **right** side facing, join next color with slip st
in first dc; ch 2, hdc in same st, work V-St in next ch-1 sp
and in each ch-1 sp across to last 2 sts, skip next
3-dc Cluster, 2 hdc in last dc; finish off: 89 V-Sts.
**Row 6:** With **wrong** side facing, join next color with slip st
in first hdc; ch 2, dc in same st, ch 1, (work 3-dc Cluster in
next ch-1 sp, ch 1) across to last 2 hdc, skip last 2 hdc,
work 2-dc Cluster in next ch; finish off: 90 ch-1 sps.
**Rows 7-97:** Repeat Rows 3-6, 22 times; then repeat
Rows 3-5 once **more**.

Holding 2 strands of **each** corresponding color together,
add additional fringe in end of each Cluster row across
*(Figs. 28b & d, page 127)*.

# PATCHWORK QUILT

*The traditional Butterfly at the Crossroads quilt pattern gives this afghan old-fashioned flair. Using granny squares and a handy placement chart, it's a snap to crochet the pretty patchwork throw.*

**Finished Size:** 46" x 64"

**MATERIALS**
Worsted Weight Yarn:
Teal - 17 ounces, (480 grams, 1,115 yards)
Lt Teal - 12 ounces, (340 grams, 790 yards)
Off-White - 9 ounces, (260 grams, 590 yards)
Crochet hook, size I (5.50 mm) **or** size needed for gauge
Yarn needle

**GAUGE:** Each Square = 3"

Referring to the Key, make the number of Squares specified in the colors indicated.

## SQUARE A

With color indicated, ch 4; join with slip st to form a ring.
**Rnd 1 (Right side):** Ch 3 **(counts as first dc, now and throughout)**, 2 dc in ring, ch 2, (3 dc in ring, ch 2) 3 times; join with slip st to first dc: 12 dc and 4 ch-2 sps.
*Note:* Loop a short piece of yarn around any stitch to mark Rnd 1 as **right** side.
**Rnd 2:** Slip st in next 2 dc and in next ch-2 sp, ch 3, (2 dc, ch 2, 3 dc) in same sp, ch 1, ★ (3 dc, ch 2, 3 dc) in next ch-2 sp, ch 1; repeat from ★ 2 times **more**; join with slip st to first dc, finish off: 24 dc and 8 sps.

## SQUARE B

With Teal, ch 4; join with slip st to form a ring.
**Rnd 1** (Right side)**:** Ch 5 **(counts as first dc plus ch 2)**, 3 dc in ring, cut Teal, with Off-White, YO and draw through, ch 1, (3 dc, ch 2, 3 dc) in ring, cut Off-White, with Teal, YO and draw through, ch 1, 2 dc in ring; join with slip st to first dc: 12 dc and 4 ch-2 sps.
*Note:* Mark Rnd 1 as **right** side.
**Rnd 2:** Slip st in first ch-2 sp, ch 3, (2 dc, ch 2, 3 dc) in same sp, ch 1, 3 dc in next ch-2 sp, cut Teal, with Off-White, YO and draw through, ch 1, 3 dc in same sp, ch 1, (3 dc, ch 2, 3 dc) in next ch-2 sp, ch 1, 3 dc in next ch-2 sp, cut Off-White, with Teal, YO and draw through, ch 1, 3 dc in same sp, ch 1; join with slip st to first dc, finish off: 24 dc and 8 sps.

## ASSEMBLY

With matching color, using Placement Diagram as a guide, and working through inside loops only, whipstitch Squares together **(Fig. 26a, page 127)**, forming 15 vertical strips of 21 Squares each, beginning in second ch of first corner ch-2 and ending in first ch of next corner ch-2; whipstitch strips together in same manner.

## EDGING

**Rnd 1:** With **right** side facing, join Off-White with sc in any corner ch-2 sp *(see Joining With Sc, page 126)*; sc in same sp, sc evenly around, working 3 sc in each corner ch-2 sp, sc in same sp as first sc; join with slip st to first sc.
**Rnd 2:** Ch 1, 3 sc in same st, sc in each sc across to center sc of next corner 3-sc group, ★ 3 sc in center sc, sc in each sc across to center sc of next corner 3-sc group; repeat from ★ 2 times **more**; join with slip st to first sc, finish off.

**PLACEMENT DIAGRAM**

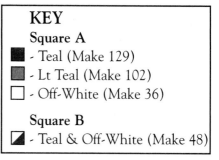

**KEY**
**Square A**
■ - Teal (Make 129)
▨ - Lt Teal (Make 102)
□ - Off-White (Make 36)

**Square B**
◩ - Teal & Off-White (Make 48)

# TEAL TAPESTRY

*A tapestry of teal, our elegant afghan makes a distinctive accent
as well as a toasty wrap. The feathery pattern is formed using
long double crochets and shells and is worked in three shades.*

**Finished Size:** 46" x 61"

## MATERIALS
Worsted Weight Yarn:
  Dk Teal - 9 ounces, (260 grams, 670 yards)
  Lt Teal - 17 ounces, (480 grams, 1,265 yards)
  Teal - 9 ounces, (260 grams, 670 yards)
Crochet hook, size I (5.50 mm) **or** size needed for gauge

**GAUGE:** Each repeat from point to point = 3¹/₂"
  and 6 rows = 4"

**Gauge Swatch:** 7"w x 4"h
Ch 41 **loosely.**
Work same as Afghan for 6 rows.
Finish off.

## STITCH GUIDE

**SHELL**
(2 Dc, ch 3, 2 dc) in st or sp indicated.
**LONG DOUBLE CROCHET** *(abbreviated LDC)*
YO, working **around** next ch-2, insert hook in st or sp
indicated one row **below**, YO and pull up a loop even
with last st made, (YO and draw through 2 loops on
hook) twice *(Fig. 17, page 123).*

## COLOR SEQUENCE
2 Rows **each:** Dk Teal *(Fig. 23a, page 126),* ★ Lt Teal,
Teal, Lt Teal, Dk Teal; repeat from ★ throughout.

With Dk Teal, ch 261 **loosely.**
**Row 1 (Right side):** Dc in fourth ch from hook **(3 skipped
chs count as first dc),** ch 2, skip next 3 chs, 2 dc in next ch,
ch 2, skip next 3 chs, work Shell in next ch, ★ (ch 2, skip
next 3 chs, 2 dc in next ch) twice, (skip next 3 chs, 2 dc in
next ch, ch 2) twice, skip next 3 chs, work Shell in next ch;
repeat from ★ 11 times **more,** ch 2, skip next 3 chs, 2 dc in
next ch, ch 2, skip next 3 chs, dc in last 2 chs: 156 dc and
65 sps.

**Row 2:** Ch 3 **(counts as first dc, now and throughout),**
turn; skip next dc, work LDC in center ch of first 3 skipped
chs on beginning ch, ch 2, skip next 2 dc, work 2 LDC in
center ch of next 3 skipped chs on beginning ch, ch 2, skip
next 2 dc, work Shell in next ch-3 sp, ★ (ch 2, skip next
2 dc, work 2 LDC in center ch of next 3 skipped chs on
beginning ch) twice, skip next 4 dc, (work 2 LDC in center
ch of next 3 skipped chs on beginning ch, ch 2, skip next
2 dc) twice, work Shell in next ch-3 sp; repeat from ★ 11
times **more,** ch 2, skip next 2 dc, work 2 LDC in center ch
of next 3 skipped chs on beginning ch, ch 2, skip next 2 dc,
work LDC in center ch of last 3 skipped chs on beginning
ch, skip next dc, dc in last dc.
**Row 3:** Ch 3, turn; skip next LDC, work 2 LDC in sp
**between** next 2 dc *(Fig. 20, page 124),* ch 2, skip next
2 LDC, work 2 LDC in sp **between** next 2 dc, ch 2, skip
next 2 dc, work Shell in next ch-3 sp, (ch 2, skip next
2 sts, work 2 LDC in sp **between** next 2 sts) twice, ★ skip
next 4 LDC, (work 2 LDC in sp **between** next 2 dc, ch 2,
skip next 2 sts) twice, work Shell in next ch-3 sp, (ch 2,
skip next 2 sts, work 2 LDC in sp **between** next 2 dc)
twice; repeat from ★ 11 times **more,** skip next LDC, dc in
last dc.
**Row 4:** Ch 3, turn; skip next 2 LDC, (work 2 LDC in sp
**between** next 2 sts, ch 2, skip next 2 sts) twice, work Shell
in next ch-3 sp, (ch 2, skip next 2 sts, work 2 LDC in sp
**between** next 2 sts) twice, ★ skip next 4 LDC, (work
2 LDC in sp **between** next 2 sts, ch 2, skip next 2 sts)
twice, work Shell in next ch-3 sp, (ch 2, skip next 2 sts,
work 2 LDC in sp **between** next 2 sts) twice; repeat from ★
11 times **more,** skip next 2 LDC, dc in last dc.
Repeat Row 4 until Afghan measures 60" from beginning
ch, ending by working one row of Dk Teal; do **not**
finish off.
**Last Row:** Ch 3, turn; skip next 2 LDC, (work 2 LDC in
sp **between** next 2 sts, sc in next 2 sts) twice, (sc, ch 3, sc)
in next ch-3 sp, (sc in next 2 sts, work 2 LDC in sp
**between** next 2 sts) twice, ★ skip next 4 LDC, (work
2 LDC in sp **between** next 2 sts, sc in next 2 sts) twice, (sc,
ch 3, sc) in next ch-3 sp, (sc in next 2 sts, work 2 LDC in
sp **between** next 2 sts) twice; repeat from ★ 11 times **more,**
skip next 2 LDC, dc in last dc; finish off.

# STRIKING STRIPES

*Like Joseph's coat of many colors, this afghan features stripes
in many striking hues. The manly wrap will look great whether
you follow our color scheme or use your scraps at random.*

**Finished Size:** 55" x 71"

## MATERIALS
Worsted Weight Yarn:
Beige - 16 ounces, (450 grams, 1,050 yards)
Teal - 13 ounces, (370 grams, 855 yards)
Dk Teal - 6 ounces, (170 grams, 395 yards)
Rust - 11 ounces, (310 grams, 725 yards)
Dk Rust - 5 ounces, (140 grams, 330 yards)
Blue - 11 ounces, (310 grams, 725 yards)
Dk Blue - 5 ounces, (140 grams, 330 yards)
Crochet hook, size H (5.00 mm) **or** size needed for gauge

**GAUGE:** In pattern, 11 sts and 11 rows = 3"

**Gauge Swatch:** 4"w x 3"h
Ch 16 **loosely.**
Work same as Afghan for 11 rows.
Finish off.

*Note:* Each row is worked across length of Afghan.
When joining yarn and finishing off, always
leave a 9" end to be worked into fringe.

With Beige, ch 262 **loosely.**
**Row 1:** Sc in second ch from hook, (dc in next ch, sc in
next ch) across: 261 sts.
**Row 2 (Right side):** Ch 1, turn; sc in each st across;
finish off: 261 sc.
*Note:* Loop a short piece of yarn around any stitch to mark
Row 2 as **right** side.
**Row 3:** With **wrong** side facing, join Teal with slip st in
first sc; ch 1, sc in same st, (tr in next sc, sc in next sc)
across pushing tr to **right** side.
**Row 4:** Ch 1, turn; sc in each st across; finish off.
**Row 5:** With **wrong** side facing, join Dk Teal with slip st
in first sc; ch 1, sc in same st, (dc in next sc, sc in next sc)
across.
**Row 6:** Ch 1, turn; sc in each st across; finish off.
**Rows 7 and 8:** Repeat Rows 3 and 4.

**Row 9:** With **wrong** side facing, join Beige with slip st in
first sc; ch 1, sc in same st, (dc in next sc, sc in next sc)
across.
**Row 10:** Ch 1, turn; sc in each st across; finish off.
**Row 11:** With **wrong** side facing, join Rust with slip st in
first sc; ch 1, sc in same st, (tr in next sc, sc in next sc)
across pushing tr to **right** side.
**Row 12:** Ch 1, turn; sc in each st across; finish off.
**Row 13:** With **wrong** side facing, join Dk Rust with slip st
in first sc; ch 1, sc in same st, (dc in next sc, sc in next sc)
across.
**Row 14:** Ch 1, turn; sc in each st across; finish off.
**Rows 15 and 16:** Repeat Rows 11 and 12.
**Row 17:** With **wrong** side facing, join Beige with slip st in
first sc; ch 1, sc in same st, (dc in next sc, sc in next sc)
across.
**Row 18:** Ch 1, turn; sc in each st across; finish off.
**Row 19:** With **wrong** side facing, join Blue with slip st in
first sc; ch 1, sc in same st, (tr in next sc, sc in next sc)
across pushing tr to **right** side.
**Row 20:** Ch 1, turn; sc in each st across; finish off.
**Row 21:** With **wrong** side facing, join Dk Blue with slip st
in first sc; ch 1, sc in same st, (dc in next sc, sc in next sc)
across.
**Row 22:** Ch 1, turn; sc in each st across; finish off.
**Rows 23 and 24:** Repeat Rows 19 and 20.
**Row 25:** With **wrong** side facing, join Beige with slip st in
first sc; ch 1, sc in same st, (dc in next sc, sc in next sc)
across.
**Row 26:** Ch 1, turn; sc in each st across; finish off.
**Rows 27-202:** Repeat Rows 3-26, 7 times; then repeat
Rows 3-10 once **more.**

Holding 4 strands of corresponding color together, add
additional fringe to beginning and ending lengths across
short edge of Afghan *(Figs. 28b & d, page 127)*.
On remaining short edge of Afghan, add fringe using
5 strands of corresponding color.

# WOODLAND WARMER

*Delight the outdoorsman with our rugged throw! Cross-stitched trees and woodland creatures are showcased on simple blocks that are whipstitched together for this cozy comforter.*

**Finished Size:** 48" x 61"

## MATERIALS

Worsted Weight Yarn:
  Ecru - 43 ounces, (1,220 grams, 2,825 yards)
  Brown - 9 ounces, (260 grams, 615 yards)
  Tan - 25 yards
  Green - 55 yards
  Black - 15 yards
Crochet hook, size H (5.00 mm) **or** size needed for gauge
Tapestry needle
Yarn needle

**GAUGE:** In pattern, (sc, ch 1) 9 times and
    17 rows = 4"
    Each Block with Edging = 12"w x 12¹/4"h

**Gauge Swatch:** 4¹/4"w x 4"h
Ch 20 **loosely.**
Work same as Block for 17 rows.
Finish off.

## STITCH GUIDE

**LONG SC *(abbreviated LSC)***
Insert hook in ch-1 sp 2 rows or 2 sts **below** row or st indicated, YO and pull up a loop even with last st made, YO and draw through both loops on hook (*Fig. 17, page 123*).
**REVERSE SINGLE CROCHET**
Working from **left** to **right**, ★ insert hook in st to right of hook, YO and draw through, under, and to left of loop on hook (2 loops on hook), YO and draw through both loops on hook; repeat from ★ around (*Figs. 19a-d, page 124*).

## BLOCK (Make 24)

With Ecru, ch 54 **loosely.**
**Row 1 (Right side):** Sc in second ch from hook, (ch 1, skip next ch, sc in next ch) across: 26 ch-1 sps.
**Note:** Loop a short piece of yarn around any stitch to mark Row 1 as **right** side.

**Row 2:** Ch 1, turn; sc in first sc and in next ch-1 sp, (ch 1, skip next sc, sc in next ch-1 sp) across to last sc, sc in last sc: 25 ch-1 sps.
**Row 3:** Ch 1, turn; sc in first sc, (ch 1, skip next sc, sc in next ch-1 sp) across to last sc, sc in last sc: 26 ch-1 sps.
**Rows 4-25:** Repeat Rows 2 and 3, 11 times.
**Row 26:** Ch 1, turn; sc in first sc and in next ch-1 sp, (ch 1, skip next sc, sc in next ch-1 sp) 13 times, place marker around last ch-1 made to mark center, (ch 1, skip next sc, sc in next ch-1 sp) across to last sc, sc in last sc: 25 ch-1 sps.
**Row 27:** Repeat Row 3.
**Rows 28-51:** Repeat Rows 2 and 3, 11 times.
Finish off.

## EDGING

With **right** side facing, join Brown with slip st in last sc on Row 51; † working in end of rows, skip first 3 rows, work (LSC, ch 1) twice in next row, (skip next row, work LSC in next row, ch 1) 21 times, skip next row, work (LSC, ch 1, LSC) in next row, skip next 3 rows †, slip st in free loop of first ch (*Fig. 25b, page 126*), skip next 2 chs; working over beginning ch, work (LSC, ch 1) twice in next ch-1 sp, (skip next ch, work LSC in next ch-1 sp, ch 1) 22 times, skip next ch, work (LSC, ch 1, LSC) in next ch-1 sp, skip next 2 chs, slip st in free loop of next ch, repeat from † to † once; working across last row, slip st in first sc, skip next ch-1 sp and next sc, (work LSC, ch 1) twice in next ch-1 sp, (skip next sc, work LSC in next ch-1 sp, ch 1) 22 times, skip next sc, work (LSC, ch 1, LSC) in next ch-1 sp, skip next sc and next ch-1 sp; join with slip st to first slip st, finish off.

## CROSS STITCH

Add cross stitch following Charts, page 125.

## ASSEMBLY

With Brown, using Placement Diagram as a guide, and working through inside loops only, whipstitch Blocks together (*Fig. 26a, page 127*), forming 4 vertical strips of 5 Blocks each, beginning in slip st of first corner and ending in slip st of next corner; whipstitch strips together in same manner.

## PLACEMENT DIAGRAM

| T | M | T | B |
|---|---|---|---|
| D | T | M | T |
| T | M | T | D |
| B | T | M | T |
| T | D | T | B |

| KEY |
|-----|
| T - Tree |
| M - Moose |
| B - Bear |
| D - Deer |

# EDGING

With **right** side facing and working in ch-1 sps, join Brown with slip st in any ch-1 sp; ch 1, working from **left** to **right**, work reverse sc evenly around *(Figs. 19a-d, page 124)*; join with slip st to first sc, finish off.

# to grandmother's
# HOUSE
## we go

Filled with nostalgic afghans, this sweet collection will recapture memories of childhood visits to Grandmother's house. Just being wrapped in one of her handmade throws made everything feel better, from a scraped knee to the rainy day blues. Reminiscent of those beloved blankets, our treasury of throws includes a variety of patterns, from frilly fancies to simple classics. Each one is sure to revive fond recollections of bygone days.

# BLUE & WHITE CHINA

*Worked in blue and white granny squares to resemble old-fashioned china,*
*this timeless afghan is a warm reminder of dinnertime at Grandmother's.*
*The fanciful throw is finished with a delicate picot edging.*

**Finished Size:** 50½" x 67"

## MATERIALS

Worsted Weight Yarn:
Dk Blue - 2½ ounces, (70 grams, 165 yards)
Med Blue - 7½ ounces, (210 grams, 495 yards)
Blue - 5 ounces, (140 grams, 330 yards)
Lt Blue - 7½ ounces, (210 grams, 495 yards)
White - 20 ounces, (570 grams, 1,315 yards)
Crochet hook, size G (4.00 mm) **or** size needed for gauge

**GAUGE:** Each Square = 8¼"

**Gauge Swatch:** 4¾"
Work same as Rnds 1-4.
Finish off.

## STITCH GUIDE

> **PICOT**
> Ch 3, slip st in top of last sc made.

## FIRST SQUARE

With Dk Blue, ch 4; join with slip st to form a ring.
**Rnd 1 (Right side):** Ch 4 **(counts as first tr, now and throughout)**, 15 tr in ring; join with slip st to first tr, finish off: 16 tr.
*Note:* Loop a short piece of yarn around any stitch to mark Rnd 1 as **right** side.
**Rnd 2:** With **right** side facing, join Med Blue with sc in any tr *(see Joining With Sc, page 126)*; ch 4, skip next tr, (sc in next tr, ch 4, skip next tr) around; join with slip st to first sc: 8 ch-4 sps.
**Rnd 3:** Slip st in first ch-4 sp, ch 4, 4 tr in same sp, ch 1, (5 tr in next ch-4 sp, ch 1) around; join with slip st to first tr, finish off: 40 tr.
**Rnd 4:** With **right** side facing, join Blue with sc in any ch-1 sp; ch 4, skip next 2 tr, sc in next tr, ch 4, ★ sc in next ch-1 sp, ch 4, skip next 2 tr, sc in next tr, ch 4; repeat from ★ around; join with slip st to first sc: 16 ch-4 sps.
**Rnd 5:** Slip st in first ch-4 sp, ch 1, sc in same sp, ch 4, (sc in next ch-4 sp, ch 4) around; join with slip st to first sc, finish off.
**Rnd 6:** With **right** side facing, join Lt Blue with slip st in last ch-4 sp made; ch 4, 8 tr in same sp, ch 1, sc in next ch-4 sp, (ch 4, sc in next ch-4 sp) twice, ch 1, ★ 9 tr in

next ch-4 sp, ch 1, sc in next ch-4 sp, (ch 4, sc in next ch-4 sp) twice, ch 1; repeat from ★ 2 times **more**; join with slip st to first tr, finish off: 48 sts and 16 sps.
**Rnd 7:** With **right** side facing, join White with sc in first tr to left of joining; ch 5, skip next 2 tr, (sc, ch 5) twice in next tr, skip next 2 tr, sc in next tr, ch 5, (sc in next ch-4 sp, ch 5) twice, ★ skip next tr, sc in next tr, ch 5, skip next 2 tr, (sc, ch 5) twice in next tr, skip next 2 tr, sc in next tr, ch 5, (sc in next ch-4 sp, ch 5) twice; repeat from ★ 2 times **more**; join with slip st to first sc: 24 ch-5 sps.
**Rnd 8:** Slip st in first ch-5 sp, ch 3 **(counts as first dc)**, 2 dc in same sp, ch 1, (3 dc, ch 2, 3 dc) in next ch-5 sp, ch 1, ★ (3 dc in next ch-5 sp, ch 1) 5 times, (3 dc, ch 2, 3 dc) in next ch-5 sp, ch 1; repeat from ★ 2 times **more**, (3 dc in next ch-5 sp, ch 1) 4 times; join with slip st to first dc: 84 dc.
**Rnd 9:** Slip st in next 2 dc and in next ch-1 sp, ch 1, sc in same sp, ch 5, (sc, ch 7, sc) in next corner ch-2 sp, ch 5, ★ (sc in next ch-1 sp, ch 5) 6 times, (sc, ch 7, sc) in next corner ch-2 sp, ch 5; repeat from ★ 2 times **more**, (sc in next ch-1 sp, ch 5) 5 times; join with slip st to first sc, finish off: 32 sps.

## ADDITIONAL SQUARES

**Rnds 1-8:** Work same as First Square: 84 dc.
**Rnd 9 (Joining rnd):** Work One or Two Side Joining, arranging Squares into 6 rows of 8 Squares each.

## ONE SIDE JOINING

**Rnd 9:** Slip st in next 2 dc and in next ch-1 sp, ch 1, sc in same sp, ch 5, † (sc, ch 7, sc) in next corner ch-2 sp, ch 5, (sc in next ch-1 sp, ch 5) 6 times †, repeat from † to † once **more**, sc in next corner ch-2 sp, ch 3; holding Squares with **wrong** sides together, slip st in center ch of corresponding corner ch-7 on **adjacent** Square *(Fig. 21, page 124)*, ch 3, sc in same sp on **new** Square, ch 2, slip st in center ch of next ch-5 on **adjacent** Square, ch 2, ★ sc in next ch-1 sp on **new** Square, ch 2, slip st in center ch of next ch-5 on **adjacent** Square, ch 2; repeat from ★ across to next corner ch-2 sp on **new** Square, sc in corner ch-2 sp, ch 3, slip st in center ch of next corner ch-7 on **adjacent** Square, ch 3, sc in same sp on **new** Square, ch 5, (sc in next ch-1 sp, ch 5) across; join with slip st to first sc, finish off.

## TWO SIDE JOINING

**Rnd 9:** Slip st in next 2 dc and in next ch-1 sp, ch 1, sc in same sp, ch 5, (sc, ch 7, sc) in next corner ch-2 sp, ch 5, (sc in next ch-1 sp, ch 5) 6 times, sc in next corner ch-2 sp,

ch 3; holding Squares with **wrong** sides together, slip st in center ch of corresponding corner ch-7 on **adjacent Square**, ★ ch 3, sc in same sp on **new Square**, ch 2, slip st in center ch of next ch-5 on **adjacent Square**, ch 2, (sc in next ch-1 sp on **new Square**, ch 2, slip st in center ch of next ch-5 on **adjacent Square**, ch 2) across to next corner ch-2 sp on **new Square**, sc in corner ch-2 sp, ch 3, slip st in same ch of corner ch-7 as joining of previous Squares; repeat from ★ once **more**, ch 3, sc in same sp on **new Square**, ch 5, (sc in next ch-1 sp, ch 5) across; join with slip st to first sc, finish off.

# EDGING

**Rnd 1:** With **right** side facing, join White with sc in any corner ch-7 sp; ch 7, sc in same sp, ch 5, (sc in next sp, ch 5) across to next corner ch-7 sp, ★ (sc, ch 7, sc) in corner sp, ch 5, (sc in next sp, ch 5) across to next corner ch-7 sp; repeat from ★ 2 times **more**; join with slip st to first sc.
**Rnd 2:** Ch 1, ★ (3 sc, work Picot, 3 sc) in corner ch-7 sp, 4 sc in each ch-5 sp across to next corner ch-7 sp; repeat from ★ around; join with slip st to first sc, finish off.

# SUMMER LACE

*Creamy motifs bordered with mauve give this dreamy summertime afghan a feeling of yesteryear. The lacy pattern is a breeze to create.*

**Finished Size:** 51" x 67"

## MATERIALS
Worsted Weight Yarn:
Off-White - 30 ounces, (850 grams, 1,900 yards)
Mauve - 18 ounces, (510 grams, 1,140 yards)
Crochet hook, size I (5.50 mm) **or** size needed for gauge
Yarn needle

**GAUGE:** Each Square = 8"

**Gauge Swatch:** 5¼"
Work same as Square Rnds 1-4.
Finish off.

## STITCH GUIDE

**DOUBLE TREBLE CROCHET (abbreviated dtr)**
YO 3 times, insert hook in sc indicated, YO and pull up a loop, (YO and draw through 2 loops on hook) 4 times **(Figs. 8a & b, page 121)**.
**CLUSTER** (uses next 3 dc)
★ YO, insert hook in **next** dc, YO and pull up a loop, YO and draw through 2 loops on hook; repeat from ★ 2 times **more**, YO and draw through all 4 loops on hook **(Figs. 16c & d, page 123)**.

## SQUARE (Make 48)
**Rnd 1 (Right side):** With Off-White, ch 8, dc in eighth ch from hook, (ch 4, dc in same ch) 6 times, ch 1, dc in fourth ch of beginning ch-8 to form last ch-4 sp: 8 ch-4 sps.
*Note:* Loop a short piece of yarn around any stitch to mark Rnd 1 as **right** side.
**Rnd 2:** Ch 1, sc in same sp, (ch 6, sc in next ch-4 sp) around, ch 2, tr in first sc to form last ch-6 sp.
**Rnd 3:** Ch 1, (sc, ch 4) twice in same sp and in each ch-6 sp around; join with slip st to first sc: 16 ch-4 sps.
**Rnd 4:** Slip st in first ch-4 sp, ch 3 **(counts as first dc, now and throughout)**, 6 dc in same sp, sc in next ch-4 sp, (7 dc in next ch-4 sp, sc in next ch-4 sp) around; join with slip st to first dc: 64 sts.
**Rnd 5:** Slip st in next 3 dc, ch 1, sc in same st, ★ † ch 5, skip next 3 dc, hdc in next sc, ch 5, skip next 3 dc, sc in next dc, ch 5, skip next 3 dc, (dtr, ch 7, dtr) in next sc †, ch 5, skip next 3 dc, sc in next dc; repeat from ★ 2 times **more**, then repeat from † to † once, ch 1, tr in first sc to form last ch-5 sp: 20 sps.
**Rnd 6:** Ch 3, 2 dc in same sp, ch 1, (3 dc in next ch-5 sp, ch 1) 3 times, (3 dc, ch 3, 3 dc) in next ch-7 sp, ch 1, ★ (3 dc in next ch-5 sp, ch 1) 4 times, (3 dc, ch 3, 3 dc) in next ch-7 sp, ch 1; repeat from ★ 2 times **more**; join with slip st to first dc, finish off: 72 dc and 24 sps.
**Rnd 7:** With **right** side facing, join Mauve with slip st in any corner ch-3 sp; ch 3, (2 dc, ch 3, 3 dc) in same sp, ch 1, (3 dc in next ch-1 sp, ch 1) 5 times, ★ (3 dc, ch 3, 3 dc) in next ch-3 sp, ch 1, (3 dc in next ch-1 sp, ch 1) 5 times; repeat from ★ 2 times **more**; join with slip st to first dc, finish off: 84 dc and 28 sps.

## ASSEMBLY
Using Mauve and working through both loops, whipstitch Squares together **(Fig. 26b, page 127)**, forming 6 vertical strips of 8 Squares each, beginning in center ch of first corner ch-3 and ending in center ch of next corner ch-3; whipstitch strips together in same manner.

## BORDER
**Rnd 1:** With **right** side facing, join Mauve with slip st in any corner ch-3 sp; ch 6, dc in same sp, ch 1, ★ † (dc in next 3 dc, ch 1) 7 times, [dc in next joining, ch 1, (dc in next 3 dc, ch 1) 7 times] across to next corner ch-3 sp †, (dc, ch 3, dc) in corner ch-3 sp, ch 1; repeat from ★ 2 times **more**, then repeat from † to † once; join with slip st to third ch of beginning ch-6: 620 sts and 4 ch-3 sps.
**Rnd 2:** Ch 2, YO, insert hook in first corner ch-3 sp, YO and pull up a loop, YO and draw through 2 loops on hook, YO, insert hook in **same** sp, YO and pull up a loop, YO and draw through 2 loops on hook, YO and draw through all 3 loops on hook, ★ † ch 5, (YO, insert hook in **same** sp, YO and pull up a loop, YO and draw through 2 loops on hook) twice, YO, insert hook in next dc, YO and pull up a loop, YO and draw through 2 loops on hook, YO and draw through all 4 loops on hook, ch 3, (work Cluster, ch 3) 7 times †, [dc in next dc, ch 3, (work Cluster, ch 3) 7 times] across to within one dc of next corner ch-3 sp, YO, insert hook in next dc, YO and pull up a loop, YO and draw through 2 loops on hook, YO, insert hook in corner ch-3 sp, YO and pull up a loop, YO and draw through 2 loops on hook, YO, insert hook in **same** sp, YO and pull up a loop, YO and

draw through 2 loops on hook, YO and draw through all 4 loops on hook; repeat from ★ 2 times **more**, then repeat from † to † once, [dc in next dc, ch 3, (work Cluster, ch 3) 7 times] across; join with slip st to top of first st: 228 sps.

**Rnd 3:** ★ Slip st in corner ch-5 sp, (ch 3, slip st in same sp) 3 times, ch 1, [(slip st, ch 3, slip st) in next ch-3 sp, ch 1] across to next corner ch-5 sp; repeat from ★ around; join with slip st to first slip st, finish off.

# GRANNY'S ROSE GARDEN

*Alternating blocks bloom with popcorn stitch "petals" on this vintage rose garden throw. A handy placement diagram makes it easy to assemble the trelliswork of squares and half squares.*

**Finished Size:** 51" x 70"

## MATERIALS
Worsted Weight Yarn:
  White - 32¹/₂ ounces, (920 grams, 2,040 yards)
  Rose - 8 ounces, (230 grams, 505 yards)
  Dk Rose - 23 ounces, (650 grams, 1,445 yards)
Crochet hook, size G (4.00 mm) **or** size needed for gauge
Yarn needle

**GAUGE:** Each Square = 4¹/₂"

## STITCH GUIDE

> **BEGINNING POPCORN**
> Ch 3, 3 dc in same sp, drop loop from hook, insert hook in top of beginning ch-3, hook dropped loop and draw through **(Fig. 14, page 122)**.
> **POPCORN**
> 4 Dc in sp indicated, drop loop from hook, insert hook in first dc of 4-dc group, hook dropped loop and draw through.
> **DC DECREASE** (uses next 2 ch-sps)
> ★ YO, insert hook in **next** ch-sp, YO and pull up a loop, YO and draw through 2 loops on hook; repeat from ★ once **more**, YO and draw through all 3 loops on hook **(counts as one dc)**.
> **SC DECREASE** (uses next 5 dc)
> Pull up a loop in **next** dc, skip next 3 dc, pull up a loop in **next** dc, YO and draw through all 3 loops on hook **(counts as one sc)**.

## SQUARE A (Make 88)
With White, ch 10; join with slip st to form a ring.
**Rnd 1** (Right side): Ch 4 **(counts as first dc plus ch 1, now and throughout)**, (dc in ring, ch 1) 15 times; join with slip st to first dc: 16 dc.
*Note:* Loop a short piece of yarn around any stitch to mark Rnd 1 as **right** side.
**Rnd 2:** Slip st in first ch-1 sp, work beginning Popcorn, (ch 1, work Popcorn in next ch-1 sp) 3 times, ch 3, ★ work Popcorn in next ch-1 sp, (ch 1, work Popcorn in next ch-1 sp) 3 times, ch 3; repeat from ★ around; join with slip st to top of beginning Popcorn, finish off: 16 Popcorns and 4 ch-3 sps.

**Rnd 3:** With **right** side facing, join Rose with slip st in any ch-3 sp; ch 3 **(counts as first dc, now and throughout)**, (3 dc, ch 2, 4 dc) in same sp (corner made), ch 1, (dc in next ch-1 sp, ch 1) 3 times, ★ (4 dc, ch 2, 4 dc) in next ch-3 sp (corner made), ch 1, (dc in next ch-1 sp, ch 1) 3 times; repeat from ★ around; join with slip st to first dc, finish off: 44 dc and 20 sps.
**Rnd 4:** With **right** side facing, join Dk Rose with slip st in any corner ch-2 sp; ch 3, (dc, ch 3, 2 dc) in same sp, skip next dc, dc in next 3 dc, ch 1, (dc in next dc, ch 1) 3 times, dc in next 3 dc, ★ (2 dc, ch 3, 2 dc) in next corner ch-2 sp, skip next dc, dc in next 3 dc, ch 1, (dc in next dc, ch 1) 3 times, dc in next 3 dc; repeat from ★ around; join with slip st to first dc, finish off: 52 dc.

## SQUARE B (Make 70)
With White, ch 10; join with slip st to form a ring.
**Rnd 1** (Right side): Ch 4, (dc in ring, ch 1) 15 times; join with slip st to first dc: 16 dc.
*Note:* Mark Rnd 1 as **right** side.
**Rnd 2:** Slip st in first ch-1 sp, ch 6 **(counts as first dc plus ch 3, now and throughout)**, ★ dc in next ch-1 sp, (ch 1, dc in next ch-1 sp) 3 times, ch 3; repeat from ★ 2 times **more**, (dc in next ch-1 sp, ch 1) 3 times; join with slip st to first dc: 16 dc and 4 ch-3 sps.
**Rnd 3:** Slip st in first ch-3 sp, ch 3, (3 dc, ch 2, 4 dc) in same sp (corner made), ch 1, (dc in next ch-1 sp, ch 1) 3 times, ★ (4 dc, ch 2, 4 dc) in next ch-3 sp (corner made), ch 1, (dc in next ch-1 sp, ch 1) 3 times; repeat from ★ around; join with slip st to first dc, finish off: 44 dc and 20 sps.
**Rnd 4:** With **right** side facing, join Dk Rose with slip st in any corner ch-2 sp; ch 3, (dc, ch 3, 2 dc) in same sp, skip next dc, dc in next 3 dc, ch 1, (dc in next dc, ch 1) 3 times, dc in next 3 dc, ★ (2 dc, ch 3, 2 dc) in next corner ch-2 sp, skip next dc, dc in next 3 dc, ch 1, (dc in next dc, ch 1) 3 times, dc in next 3 dc; repeat from ★ around; join with slip st to first dc, finish off: 52 dc.

## HALF SQUARE (Make 20)
With White, ch 10; join with slip st to form a ring.
**Row 1** (Right side): Ch 4, dc in ring, (ch 1, dc in ring) 7 times: 9 dc and 8 ch-1 sps.
*Note:* Mark Row 1 as **right** side.
**Row 2:** Ch 6, turn; ★ dc in next ch-1 sp, (ch 1, dc in next ch-1 sp) 3 times, ch 3; repeat from ★ once **more**, dc in last dc: 10 dc and 6 ch-1 sps.

**Row 3:** Ch 3, turn; 3 dc in next ch-3 sp, ch 1, (dc in next ch-1 sp, ch 1) 3 times, (4 dc, ch 2, 4 dc) in next ch-3 sp, ch 1, (dc in next ch-1 sp, ch 1) 3 times, 3 dc in next ch-3 sp, dc in last dc; finish off: 22 dc and 9 sps.

**Row 4:** With **right** side facing, join Dk Rose with slip st in first dc; ch 3, dc in same st and in next 3 dc, ch 1, (dc in next dc, ch 1) 3 times, dc in next 3 dc, (2 dc, ch 3, 2 dc) in next ch-2 sp, skip next dc, dc in next 3 dc, ch 1, (dc in next dc, ch 1) 3 times, dc in next 3 dc, 2 dc in last dc; finish off: 26 dc.

## ASSEMBLY

With Dk Rose, using Placement Diagram, page 80, as a guide, and working through both loops, whipstitch Squares together **(Fig. 26b, page 127)**, beginning in center ch of first corner and ending in center ch of next corner; whipstitch Half Squares in place along sides, beginning in first dc to left of first corner ch-3 sp and ending in last dc before next corner ch-3 sp (leave outer ch-3 sps on Squares unsewn).

Continued on page 80

# EDGING

**Rnd 1:** With **right** side facing, join Dk Rose with slip st in top right corner ch-3 sp **(point A)**; ch 6, dc in same sp, † dc in next 5 dc and in next ch-1 sp, (dc in next dc and in next ch-1 sp) 3 times, dc in next 5 dc, ★ dc decrease, dc in next 5 dc and in next ch-1 sp, (dc in next dc and in next ch-1 sp) 3 times, dc in next 5 dc, (dc, ch 3, dc) in next ch-3 sp, dc in next 5 dc and in next ch-1 sp, (dc in next dc and in next ch-1 sp) 3 times, dc in next 5 dc; repeat from ★ 6 times **more**, ch 3, skip next ch-3 sp; working in end of rows, work 22 dc evenly spaced across next Half Square, (2 dc in next ch-3 sp, work 22 dc evenly spaced across next Half Square) 9 times, ch 3, skip next ch-3 sp, dc in next 5 dc and in next ch-1 sp, (dc in next dc and next ch-1 sp) 3 times, dc in next 5 dc †, (dc, ch 3, dc) in next ch-3 sp, repeat from † to † once; join with slip st to first dc, finish off: 1,066 dc.

**Rnd 2:** With **right** side facing, join White with slip st in top right corner ch-3 sp; ch 1, (sc in same sp, ch 2) 3 times, † ★ sc in next dc, (ch 2, skip next dc, sc in next dc) 7 times, ch 2, skip next dc, sc decrease, (ch 2, skip next dc, sc in next dc) 8 times, ch 2, (sc, ch 2) 3 times in next ch-3 sp; repeat from ★ 6 times **more**, (sc in next dc, ch 2, skip next dc) 9 times, (sc, ch 2) 3 times in next ch-3 sp, (sc in next dc, ch 2, skip next dc) across to next ch-3 sp, (sc, ch 2) 3 times in ch-3 sp, skip next dc, sc in next dc, (ch 2, skip next dc, sc in next dc) 8 times, ch 2 †, (sc, ch 2) 3 times in next ch-3 sp, repeat from † to † once; join with slip st to first sc, finish off.

## PLACEMENT DIAGRAM

# PARLOR FANS

*Ideal for a quiet afternoon of reading, this plush afghan is worked in rows of fans, shells, and V-stitches. Generous fringe finishes the genteel cover-up.*

**Finished Size:** 51" x 68"

## MATERIALS
Worsted Weight Yarn:
   65 ounces, (1,850 grams, 3,140 yards)
   Crochet hook, size I (5.50 mm) **or** size needed for gauge

**GAUGE SWATCH:** 5³⁄₄"w x 4"h
Ch 26 **loosely.**
Work same as Afghan for 8 rows.
Finish off.

## STITCH GUIDE

> **FAN**
> 9 Dc in st indicated.
> **V-ST**
> (Dc, ch 1, dc) in st indicated.
> **SHELL**
> 5 Dc in st or sp indicated.

Ch 226 **loosely.**

**Row 1** (Right side): Sc in second ch from hook, ★ skip next 3 chs, work Fan in next ch, skip next 3 chs, sc in next ch; repeat from ★ across: 28 Fans.

**Row 2:** Ch 3 **(counts as first dc, now and throughout)**, turn; dc in same st, ch 5, skip next Fan, ★ work V-St in next sc, ch 5, skip next Fan; repeat from ★ across to last sc, 2 dc in last sc: 27 V-Sts.

**Row 3:** Ch 3, turn; 2 dc in same st, working **around** ch-5, sc in center dc of next Fan **below** ch-5, ★ work Shell in next V-St (ch-1 sp), working **around** ch-5, sc in center dc of next Fan **below** ch-5; repeat from ★ across to last 2 dc, skip next dc, 3 dc in last dc: 27 Shells.

**Row 4:** Turn; slip st in first dc, ch 2, skip next 2 dc, work V-St in next sc, ★ ch 5, skip next Shell, work V-St in next sc; repeat from ★ across to last 3 dc, ch 2, skip next 2 dc, slip st in last dc: 28 V-Sts.

**Row 5:** Ch 1, turn; sc in first slip st, work Fan in next V-St, ★ working **around** ch-5, sc in center dc of next Shell **below**

ch-5, work Fan in next V-St; repeat from ★ across to last slip st, sc in last slip st: 28 Fans.

Repeat Rows 2-5 until Afghan measures 66" from beginning ch, ending by working Row 5.

**Last Row:** Ch 3, turn; dc in same st, ch 2, sc in center dc of next Fan, ch 2, ★ work V-St in next sc, ch 2, sc in center dc of next Fan, ch 2; repeat from ★ across to last sc, 2 dc in last sc; do **not** finish off.

# EDGING

**Rnd 1:** Ch 1, turn; working across Last Row, 2 sc in first dc, work 195 sc evenly spaced across to last dc, 3 sc in last dc; work 255 sc evenly spaced across end of rows; working in

free loops of beginning ch *(Fig. 25b, page 126)*, 3 sc in first ch, work 195 sc evenly spaced across to ch at base of last sc, 3 sc in ch; work 255 sc evenly spaced across end of rows, sc in same st as first sc; join with slip st to first sc: 912 sc.

**Rnd 2:** Ch 2, turn; skip next 2 sc, (dc, ch 1, dc) in next sc, ch 2, skip next 2 sc, ★ slip st in next sc, ch 2, skip next 2 sc, (dc, ch 1, dc) in next sc, ch 2, skip next 2 sc; repeat from ★ around; join with slip st to base of beginning ch-2, finish off.

Holding 8 strands together and working in ch-1 sps, add fringe evenly across short edges of Afghan *(Figs. 28a & c, page 127)*.

# HONEYCOMB FLOWER PATCH

*Listening to Grandmother read a bedtime story will be even nicer when a little one is wrapped up in this flower patch pretty. A black background makes a striking contrast to the vibrant hexagon-shaped motifs.*

**Finished Size:** 46" x 64"

## MATERIALS
Worsted Weight Yarn:
Black - 24½ ounces, (700 grams, 1,385 yards)
Scraps - 25 ounces, (710 grams, 1,415 yards) **total**
Crochet hook, size H (5.00 mm) **or** size needed for gauge

**GAUGE:** Each Motif = 4"
(straight edge to straight edge)

## STITCH GUIDE

> **DECREASE** (uses next 2 chs)
> Insert hook in next ch and pull up a loop, skip joining, insert hook in next ch and pull up a loop, YO and draw through all 3 loops on hook.

## FIRST MOTIF
With first color, ch 4; join with slip st to form a ring.
**Rnd 1** (Right side)**:** Ch 3 (**counts as first dc, now and throughout**), dc in ring, ch 2, (2 dc in ring, ch 2) 5 times; join with slip st to first dc, finish off: 12 dc and 6 ch-2 sps.
*Note:* Loop a short piece of yarn around any stitch to mark Rnd 1 as **right** side.
**Rnd 2:** With **right** side facing, join next color with slip st in any ch-2 sp; ch 3, (dc, ch 2, 2 dc) in same sp, ch 1, ★ (2 dc, ch 2, 2 dc) in next ch-2 sp, ch 1; repeat from ★ around; join with slip st to first dc, finish off: 24 dc and 12 sps.
**Rnd 3:** With **right** side facing, join Black with slip st in any ch-2 sp; ch 3, (dc, ch 2, 2 dc) in same sp (corner made), ch 1, 2 dc in next ch-1 sp, ch 1, ★ (2 dc, ch 2, 2 dc) in next ch-2 sp (corner made), ch 1, 2 dc in next ch-1 sp, ch 1; repeat from ★ around; join with slip st to first dc, finish off: 36 dc and 18 sps.

## ADDITIONAL MOTIFS
With next color, ch 4; join with slip st to form a ring.
**Rnds 1 and 2:** Work same as First Motif: 24 dc and 12 sps.
**Rnd 3** (Joining rnd)**:** Following Placement Diagram, work One, Two, or Three Side Joining.

## ONE SIDE JOINING
**Rnd 3** (Joining rnd)**:** With **right** side facing, join Black with slip st in any ch-2 sp; ch 3, (dc, ch 2, 2 dc) in same sp (corner made), ch 1, 2 dc in next ch-1 sp, ch 1, ★ (2 dc, ch 2, 2 dc) in next ch-2 sp (corner made), ch 1, 2 dc in next ch-1 sp, ch 1; repeat from ★ 2 times **more**, 2 dc in next ch-2 sp, ch 1, holding Motifs with **wrong** sides together, slip st in corner sp on **adjacent Motif** (**Fig. 21, page 124**), ch 1, 2 dc in same sp on **new Motif**, ch 1, slip st in next ch-1 sp on **adjacent Motif**, 2 dc in next ch-1 sp on **new Motif**, ch 1, slip st in next ch-1 sp on **adjacent Motif**, 2 dc in next corner ch-2 sp on **new Motif**, ch 1, slip st in next corner sp on **adjacent Motif**, ch 1, 2 dc in same sp on **new Motif**, ch 1, 2 dc in next ch-1 sp, ch 1; join with slip st to first dc, finish off.

**PLACEMENT DIAGRAM**

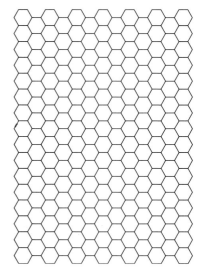

## TWO SIDE JOINING
**Rnd 3** (Joining rnd)**:** With **right** side facing, join Black with slip st in any ch-2 sp; ch 3, (dc, ch 2, 2 dc) in same sp, ch 1, 2 dc in next ch-1 sp, ch 1, ★ (2 dc, ch 2, 2 dc) in next ch-2 sp, ch 1, 2 dc in next ch-1 sp, ch 1; repeat from ★ once **more**, 2 dc in next ch-2 sp, ch 1, holding Motifs with **wrong** sides together, slip st in corner sp on **adjacent Motif**, ch 1, † 2 dc in same sp on **new Motif**, ch 1, slip st in next ch-1 sp on **adjacent Motif**, 2 dc in next ch-1 sp on **new Motif**, ch 1, slip st in next ch-1 sp on **adjacent Motif**, 2 dc in next corner ch-2 sp on **new Motif**, ch 1 †, (slip st in next corner sp on **adjacent Motif**, ch 1) twice, repeat from † to † once, slip st in next corner sp on **adjacent Motif**, ch 1, 2 dc in same sp on **new Motif**, ch 1, 2 dc in next ch-1 sp, ch 1; join with slip st to first dc, finish off.

Continued on page 84.

## THREE SIDE JOINING

**Rnd 3** (Joining rnd): With **right** side facing, join Black with slip st in any ch-2 sp; ch 3, (dc, ch 2, 2 dc) in same sp, ch 1, 2 dc in next ch-1 sp, ch 1, (2 dc, ch 2, 2 dc) in next ch-2 sp, ch 1, 2 dc in next ch-1 sp, ch 1, 2 dc in next ch-2 sp, ch 1, holding Motifs with **wrong** sides together, slip st in corner sp on **adjacent Motif**, ch 1, ★ † 2 dc in same sp on **new Motif**, ch 1, slip st in next ch-1 sp on **adjacent Motif**, 2 dc in next ch-1 sp on **new Motif**, ch 1, slip st in next ch-1 sp on **adjacent Motif**, 2 dc in next corner ch-2 sp on **new Motif**, ch 1 †, (slip st in next corner sp on **adjacent Motif**, ch 1) twice; repeat from ★ once **more**, then repeat from † to † once, slip st in next corner sp on **adjacent Motif**, ch 1, 2 dc in same sp on **new Motif**, ch 1, 2 dc in next ch-1 sp, ch 1; join with slip st to first dc, finish off.

## EDGING

With **right** side facing, join Black with slip st in first ch of any ch-2 sp; ch 1, sc in each ch and in each dc around, decreasing at each joining; join with slip st to first sc, finish off.

# OLD-FASHIONED ROSES

*The timeless beauty of roses is elegantly captured in this feminine throw. To complete the exquisite afghan, a border of delicate shell stitches is added.*

**Finished Size:** 47" x 62"

## MATERIALS
Worsted Weight Yarn:
46 ounces, (1,310 grams, 2,685 yards)
Crochet hook, size H (5.00 mm) **or** size needed for gauge
Yarn needle

**GAUGE:** Each Square = 7½"

**Gauge Swatch:** 3" in diamenter
Work same as Square Rnds 1 and 2.

## STITCH GUIDE

SHELL
(2 Dc, ch 3, 2 dc) in st indicated.

## SQUARE (Make 48)

Ch 6; join with slip st to form a ring.
**Rnd 1** (Right side): Ch 4, (dc in ring, ch 1) 11 times; join with slip st to third ch of beginning ch-4: 12 ch-1 sps.
*Note:* Loop a short piece of yarn around any stitch to mark Rnd 1 as **right** side.
**Rnd 2:** Slip st in first ch-1 sp, ch 5, dc in next ch-1 sp, (ch 2, dc in next ch-1 sp) around, ch 1, sc in third ch of beginning ch-5 to form last ch-2 sp: 12 ch-2 sps.
**Rnd 3:** Ch 1, sc in same sp, (ch 5, sc in next ch-2 sp) around, ch 2, dc in first sc to form last ch-5 sp.
**Rnd 4:** Ch 3, 2 dc in same sp, (3 dc, ch 3, 3 dc) in next ch-5 sp and in each ch-5 sp around, 3 dc in same sp as beginning ch-3, ch 1, hdc in top of beginning ch-3 to form last ch-3 sp: 72 dc.

**Rnd 5:** Ch 1, sc in same sp, (ch 6, sc in next ch-3 sp) around, ch 2, tr in first sc to form last ch-6 sp: 12 ch-6 sps.
**Rnd 6:** Ch 9, (tr, ch 3, dc) in same sp, (ch 3, sc) 3 times in each of next 2 ch-6 sps, ch 3, ★ in next ch-6 sp work (dc, ch 3, tr, ch 5, tr, ch 3, dc), (ch 3, sc) 3 times in each of next 2 ch-6 sps, ch 3; repeat from ★ around, dc in same sp as beginning ch-9, ch 1, hdc in fourth ch of beginning ch-9 to form last ch-3 sp: 40 ch-sps.
**Rnd 7:** Ch 1, sc in same sp, (ch 4, sc in next sp) around, ch 1, dc in first sc to form last ch-4 sp.
**Rnd 8:** Ch 3, 2 dc in same sp, ★ † 5 dc in next ch-4 sp, ch 3, 5 dc in next ch-4 sp, 3 dc in next ch-4 sp, 2 hdc in each of next 6 ch-4 sps †, 3 dc in next ch-4 sp; repeat from ★ 2 times **more**, then repeat from † to † once; join with slip st to top of beginning ch-3, finish off: 28 sts **each** side.

## JOINING

Working through both loops, whipstitch Squares together **(Fig. 26b, page 127)**, forming 6 vertical strips of 8 Squares each, beginning in center ch of first corner ch-3 and ending in center ch of next corner ch-3; whipstitch strips together in same manner.

## EDGING

With **right** side facing, join yarn with slip st in any corner ch-3 sp; ch 3, (3 dc, ch 3, 4 dc) in same sp, (skip next 3 sts, work Shell in next st) 6 times, ★ † skip next 4 sts, work Shell in next joining, (skip next 3 sts, work Shell in next st) 6 times †, repeat from † to † across to within 4 dc of next corner ch-3 sp, skip next 4 dc, (4 dc, ch 3, 4 dc) in corner sp, (skip next 3 sts, work Shell in next st) 6 times; repeat from ★ 2 times **more**, then repeat from † to † across to last 4 dc, skip last 4 dc; join with slip st to top of beginning ch-3, finish off.

# LICKETY-SPLIT LOG CABIN

*Worked holding two strands of yarn together, this afghan is perfect for when you need a quick-to-finish project! The classic Log Cabin quilt pattern is created with blocks stitched in three shades of blue.*

**Finished Size:** 47" x 63"

## MATERIALS

Worsted Weight Yarn:
Dk Blue - 14 ounces, (400 grams, 920 yards)
Blue - 20 ounces, (570 grams, 1,315 yards)
Lt Blue - 21 ounces, (600 grams, 1,380 yards)
Crochet hook, size N (9.00 mm) **or** size needed for gauge
Yarn needle

*Note:* Entire Afghan is worked holding two strands of yarn together.

**GAUGE:** Each Block = 7¼"w x 7½"h

## BLOCK (Make 48)

With Dk Blue, ch 4; join with slip st to form a ring.
**Rnd 1:** Ch 3 **(counts as first dc, now and throughout)**, 2 dc in ring, ch 2, (3 dc in ring, ch 2) 3 times; join with slip st to first dc: 4 ch-2 sps.
**Rnd 2** (Right side): Turn; slip st in first ch-2 sp, ch 3, 2 dc in same sp, ch 1, ★ (3 dc, ch 2, 3 dc) in next ch-2 sp, ch 1; repeat from ★ 2 times **more**, 3 dc in same sp as first dc, ch 2; join with slip st to first dc, finish off: 24 dc and 8 sps.
*Note:* Loop a short piece of yarn around any stitch to mark Rnd 2 as **right** side.
Begin working in rows.
**Row 1:** With **wrong** side facing, join Blue with slip st in any corner ch-2 sp; ch 3, 2 dc in same sp, ch 1, 3 dc in next ch-1 sp, ch 1, (3 dc, ch 2, 3 dc) in next ch-2 sp, (ch 1, 3 dc in next sp) twice, leave remaining sps unworked: 5 sps.
**Row 2:** Ch 4 **(counts as first dc plus ch 1, now and throughout)**, turn; (3 dc in next ch-1 sp, ch 1) twice, (3 dc, ch 2, 3 dc) in next ch-2 sp, ch 1, (3 dc in next ch-1 sp, ch 1) twice, skip next 2 dc, dc in last dc; finish off: 20 dc.
**Row 3:** With **wrong** side facing, join Lt Blue with slip st in first ch-1 sp; ch 3, 2 dc in same sp, ch 1, (3 dc in next ch-1 sp, ch 1) twice, (3 dc, ch 2, 3 dc) in next ch-2 sp, (ch 1, 3 dc in next ch-1 sp) 3 times: 7 sps.
**Row 4:** Ch 4, turn; (3 dc in next ch-1 sp, ch 1) 3 times, (3 dc, ch 2, 3 dc) in next ch-2 sp, ch 1, (3 dc in next ch-1 sp, ch 1) 3 times, skip next 2 dc, dc in last dc; finish off: 9 sps.

## ASSEMBLY

Using 2 strands of Lt Blue and Placement Diagram as a guide, sew Blocks together, forming 6 vertical strips of 8 Blocks each, working in end of rows and in both loops of stitches; sew strips together in same manner.

### PLACEMENT DIAGRAM

## EDGING

**Rnd 1:** With **wrong** side facing, join Blue with slip st in any corner sp; ch 3, (2 dc, ch 2, 3 dc) in same sp, ch 1, (3 dc in next sp, ch 1) across to next corner sp, ★ (3 dc, ch 2, 3 dc) in corner sp, ch 1, (3 dc in next sp, ch 1) across to next corner sp; repeat from ★ 2 times **more**; join with slip st to first dc.
**Rnd 2:** Turn; slip st in first ch-1 sp, ch 3, 2 dc in same sp, ch 1, ★ (3 dc in next ch-1 sp, ch 1) across to next corner ch-2 sp, (3 dc, ch 2, 3 dc) in corner ch-2 sp, ch 1; repeat from ★ around; join with slip st to first dc, finish off.

# PATCHWORK MEMORIES

*A blanket of fanciful pinwheels, this nostalgic wrap is a sweet reminder of simpler times and youthful pleasures. To create the afghan's patchwork quilt look, one- and two-color granny squares are whipstitched together following a placement diagram.*

**Finished Size:** 48" x 69"

## MATERIALS

Worsted Weight Yarn:
   Green - 28 ounces, (800 grams, 1,840 yards)
   Off-White - 14 ounces, (400 grams, 920 yards)
   Peach - 7 ounces, (200 grams, 460 yards)
   Blue - 7 ounces, (200 grams, 460 yards)
Crochet hook, size I (5.50 mm) **or** size needed for gauge
Yarn needle

**GAUGE:** Each Square = 3"

## STITCH GUIDE

> **DOUBLE TREBLE CROCHET (abbreviated dtr)**
> YO 3 times, insert hook in sc indicated, YO and pull up a loop, (YO and draw through 2 loops on hook) 4 times (*Figs. 8a & b, page 121*).

Referring to the Key, make the number of Squares specified in the colors indicated.

## SQUARE A

With color indicated, ch 4; join with slip st to form a ring.
**Rnd 1 (Right side):** Ch 3 (**counts as first dc, now and throughout**), 2 dc in ring, ch 2, (3 dc in ring, ch 2) 3 times; join with slip st to first dc: 12 dc and 4 ch-2 sps.
**Note:** Loop a short piece of yarn around any stitch to mark Rnd 1 as **right** side.
**Rnd 2:** Slip st in next 2 dc and in next ch-2 sp, ch 3, (2 dc, ch 2, 3 dc) in same sp, ch 1, ★ (3 dc, ch 2, 3 dc) in next ch-2 sp, ch 1; repeat from ★ 2 times **more**; join with slip st to first dc, finish off: 24 dc and 8 sps.

## SQUARE B

With first color, ch 4; join with slip st to form a ring.
**Rnd 1 (Right side):** Ch 5 (**counts as first dc plus ch 2**), 3 dc in ring, cut first color, with second color, YO and draw through, ch 1, (3 dc, ch 2, 3 dc) in ring, cut second color, with first color, YO and draw through, ch 1, 2 dc in ring; join with slip st to first dc: 12 dc and 4 ch-2 sps.
**Note:** Mark Rnd 1 as **right** side.
**Rnd 2:** Slip st in first ch-2 sp, ch 3, (2 dc, ch 2, 3 dc) in same sp, ch 1, 3 dc in next ch-2 sp, cut first color, with second color, YO and draw through, ch 1, 3 dc in same sp, ch 1, (3 dc, ch 2, 3 dc) in next ch-2 sp, ch 1, 3 dc in next ch-2 sp, cut second color, with first color, YO and draw through, ch 1, 3 dc in same sp, ch 1; join with slip st to first dc, finish off: 24 dc and 8 sps.

## ASSEMBLY

With matching color, using Placement Diagram, page 90, as a guide, and working through inside loops only, whipstitch Squares together (*Fig. 26a, page 127*), forming 15 vertical strips of 22 Squares each, beginning in second ch of first corner ch-2 and ending in first ch of next corner ch-2; whipstitch strips together in same manner.

## EDGING

**Rnd 1:** With **right** side facing and working across short edge of Afghan, join Green with sc in top right corner ch-2 sp (*see Joining With Sc, page 126*); sc in same sp, sc in each dc and in each sp and joining across to next corner ch-2 sp, ★ 3 sc in corner ch-2 sp, sc in each dc and in each sp and joining across to next corner ch-2 sp; repeat from ★ 2 times **more**, sc in same sp as first sc; join with slip st to first sc: 740 sc.
**Rnd 2:** Ch 1, 2 sc in same st, ★ † sc in next sc, hdc in next sc, dc in next sc, tr in next sc, dtr in next sc, tr in next sc, dc in next sc, hdc in next sc, sc in next sc, ♥ slip st in next sc, sc in next sc, hdc in next sc, dc in next sc, tr in next sc, dtr in next sc, tr in next sc, dc in next sc, hdc in next sc, sc in next sc ♥, repeat from ♥ to ♥ across to center sc of next corner 3-sc group †, 3 sc in center sc; repeat from ★ 2 times **more**, then repeat from † to † once, sc in same st as first sc; join with slip st to first sc: 748 sts.

Continued on page 90.

**Rnd 3:** Ch 1, 3 sc in same st, † sc in next 5 sts, 3 sc in next dtr, (sc in next 9 sts, 3 sc in next dtr) 14 times, sc in next 5 sts, 3 sc in next sc, sc in next 5 sts, 3 sc in next dtr, (sc in next 9 sts, 3 sc in next dtr) 21 times, sc in next 5 sts †, 3 sc in next sc, repeat from † to † once; join with slip st to first sc, finish off.

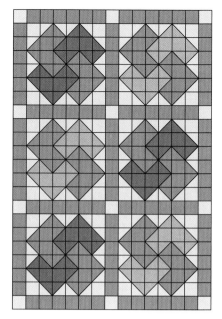

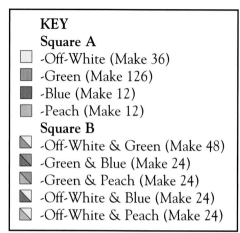

**KEY**
**Square A**
☐ -Off-White (Make 36)
▨ -Green (Make 126)
■ -Blue (Make 12)
▨ -Peach (Make 12)
**Square B**
◸ -Off-White & Green (Make 48)
◸ -Green & Blue (Make 24)
◸ -Green & Peach (Make 24)
◸ -Off-White & Blue (Make 24)
◸ -Off-White & Peach (Make 24)

# AIRY HEIRLOOM

*Created with brushed acrylic yarn, this soft filigree fancy is a treasured heirloom in the making. The airy afghan is worked in lacy strips for fast assembly.*

**Finished Size:** 48" x 69"

## MATERIALS
Worsted Weight Brushed Acrylic Yarn:
31 ounces, (880 grams, 2,390 yards)
Crochet hook, size H (5.00 mm) **or** size needed for gauge

**GAUGE:** Each Strip = 6" wide

# STRIP (Make 8)
Ch 21.
**Row 1 (Right side):** (2 Dc, ch 2, 2 dc) in seventh ch from hook, ch 5, skip next 6 chs, (dc, ch 2, dc) in next ch, ch 5, skip next 6 chs, (2 dc, ch 2, 2 dc) in last ch: 10 dc and 3 ch-2 sps.
*Note:* Loop a short piece of yarn around any stitch to mark Row 1 as **right** side and bottom edge.
**Row 2:** Ch 5, turn; (2 dc, ch 2, 2 dc) in first ch-2 sp, ch 4, skip next ch-5 sp, 5 dc in next ch-2 sp, ch 4, skip next ch-5 sp, (2 dc, ch 2, 2 dc) in last ch-2 sp: 13 dc.
**Row 3:** Ch 5, turn; (2 dc, ch 2, 2 dc) in first ch-2 sp, skip next 2 dc, 2 dc in each of next 2 dc, 3 dc in next dc, 2 dc in each of next 2 dc, (2 dc, ch 2, 2 dc) in last ch-2 sp: 19 dc.

**Row 4:** Ch 5, turn; (2 dc, ch 2, 2 dc) in first ch-2 sp, skip next 3 dc, dc in next dc, ch 2, hdc in post of dc just made *(Fig. 13, page 122)*, ★ ch 1, skip next dc, dc in next dc, ch 2, hdc in post of dc just made; repeat from ★ 3 times **more**, (2 dc, ch 2, 2 dc) in last ch-2 sp: 13 dc and 7 ch-2 sps.
**Row 5:** Ch 5, turn; (2 dc, ch 2, 2 dc) in first ch-2 sp, ch 5, skip next 2 ch-2 sps, (dc, ch 2, dc) in next ch-2 sp, ch 5, skip next 2 ch-2 sps, (2 dc, ch 2, 2 dc) in last ch-2 sp: 10 dc and 3 ch-2 sps.
Repeat Rows 2-5 until Strip measures 69" from beginning ch, ending by working Row 4.
Finish off.

# JOINING
Place two Strips with **right** sides together and bottom edges at the same end. Join yarn with slip st in first ch-5 sp in end of Row 1 on **back** Strip; ch 3, sc in first sp on **front** Strip *(Fig. 21, page 124)*, ch 3, ★ sc in next ch-5 sp on **back** Strip, ch 3, sc in next ch-5 sp on **front** Strip, ch 3; repeat from ★ across, slip st in last dc on **back** Strip; finish off. Join remaining Strips in same manner.

# QUEEN'S TRELLIS

*This blanket of cluster stitches is reminiscent of the prized afghans Grandmother would display for Sunday afternoon company. Elegant satin ribbon is interwoven through the lacy edging, and regal tassels accent each corner of the formal throw.*

**Finished Size:** 47" x 60"

## MATERIALS
Worsted Weight Yarn:
  49 ounces, (1,390 grams, 2,860 yards)
Crochet hooks, size G (4.00 mm) **and** K (6.50 mm) **or**
  sizes needed for gauge
Yarn needle
11 yards of ³/8" ribbon

**GAUGE:** For Center, with small size hook, in pattern,
  37 sts = 10" and 8 rows = 4"
  For Edging, with large size hook, 12 sc = 4"

**Gauge Swatch:** 10"w x 4"h
Ch 38 **loosely.**
Work same as Center for 8 rows.
Finish off.

## STITCH GUIDE

### CLUSTER
★ YO, insert hook in st indicated, YO and pull up a loop, YO and draw through 2 loops on hook; repeat from ★ once **more,** YO and draw through all 3 loops on hook *(Figs. 16a & b, page 123).*
### DOUBLE CLUSTER *(uses same st and next st)*
(YO, insert hook in **same** st, YO and pull up a loop, YO and draw through 2 loops on hook) twice, YO, insert hook in **next** st, YO and pull up a loop, YO and draw through 2 loops on hook, YO, insert hook in **same** st, YO and pull up a loop, YO and draw through 2 loops on hook, YO and draw through all 5 loops on hook *(Figs. 16c & d, page 123).*
### TRIPLE TREBLE CROCHET *(abbreviated Tr tr)*
YO 4 times, insert hook in st indicated, YO and pull up a loop, (YO and draw through 2 loops on hook) 5 times *(Figs. 9a & b, page 121).*
### 3-PICOT GROUP
(Ch 6, slip st, ch 8, slip st, ch 6, slip st) in top of last dc made.

## CENTER
With small size hook, ch 128 **loosely.**
**Row 1 (Right side):** Sc in second ch from hook, ★ skip next 2 chs, 5 dc in next ch, skip next 2 chs, sc in next ch; repeat from ★ across: 21 5-dc groups.
**Note:** Loop a short piece of yarn around any stitch to mark Row 1 as **right** side.
**Row 2:** Ch 3 **(counts as first dc, now and throughout),** turn; 2 dc in same st, ch 1, skip next 2 dc, sc in next dc, ch 1, skip next 2 dc and next sc, work Cluster in next dc, ch 2, (work Double Cluster, ch 2) 4 times, work Cluster in same st, ch 1, skip next sc and next 2 dc, sc in next dc, ch 1, ★ skip next 2 dc, 5 dc in next sc, ch 1, skip next 2 dc, sc in next dc, ch 1, skip next 2 dc and next sc, work Cluster in next dc, ch 2, (work Double Cluster, ch 2) 4 times, work Cluster in same st, ch 1, skip next sc and next 2 dc, sc in next dc, ch 1; repeat from ★ across to last 3 sts, skip next 2 dc, 3 dc in last sc.
**Row 3:** Ch 1, turn; sc in first dc, ch 2, work Cluster in next Cluster, ch 2, (work Double Cluster, ch 2) 5 times, work Cluster in same st, ch 2, ★ skip next sc and next 2 dc, sc in next dc, ch 2, work Cluster in next Cluster, ch 2, (work Double Cluster, ch 2) 5 times, work Cluster in same st, ch 2; repeat from ★ across to last 4 sts, skip next sc and next 2 dc, sc in last dc.
**Row 4:** Ch 1, turn; sc in first sc, ★ 2 sc in next ch-2 sp, (sc in next Cluster, 2 sc in next ch-2 sp) 7 times, sc in next sc; repeat from ★ across: 169 sc.
**Row 5:** Ch 1, turn; sc in first sc, ★ ch 1, skip next 3 sc, 5 dc in next sc, ch 1, skip next 3 sc, sc in next sc; repeat from ★ across: 21 5-dc groups.
Repeat Rows 2-5 until Center measures 48" from beginning ch, ending by working Row 5.
Do **not** finish off.

## EDGING
Change to large size hook.
**Rnd 1:** Ch 1, do **not** turn; work 145 sc evenly spaced across end of rows, 4 sc in free loop of first ch *(Fig. 25b, page 126)*; working over beginning ch, work 105 sc evenly spaced across to ch at base of last sc, 4 sc in free loop of ch; work 145 sc evenly spaced across end of rows; working in sts across last row, 4 sc in first sc, work 105 sc evenly spaced across to last sc, 4 sc in last sc; join with slip st to Back Loop Only of first sc *(Fig. 24, page 126)*: 516 sc.

**Rnd 2** (Eyelet rnd): Ch 4, working in Back Loops Only, skip next sc, dc in next sc, (ch 1, skip next sc, dc in next sc) 72 times, ch 1 (corner made), dc in next sc, (ch 1, skip next sc, dc in next sc) 54 times, ch 1 (corner made), dc in next sc, (ch 1, skip next sc, dc in next sc) 74 times, ch 1 (corner made), dc in next sc, (ch 1, skip next sc, dc in next sc) 54 times, ch 1 (corner made), dc in next sc, ch 1, skip last sc; join with slip st to third ch of beginning ch-4: 260 ch-1 sps.

**Rnd 3:** Ch 1, sc in same st, ★ sc in each ch-1 sp and in each dc across to next corner ch-1 sp, 3 sc in ch-1 sp; repeat from ★ 3 times **more**, sc in next dc and in last ch-1 sp; join with slip st to first sc: 528 sc.
Change to small size hook.

**Rnd 4:** Ch 1, sc in same st, ch 7, (skip next sc, sc in next sc, ch 7) 4 times, † (skip next 2 sc, sc in next sc, ch 7) 46 times, (skip next 3 sc, sc in next sc, ch 7) 4 times, (skip next 2 sc, sc in next sc, ch 7) 32 times, skip next 3 sc, sc in next sc, ch 7 †, (skip next sc, sc in next sc, ch 7) 5 times, repeat from † to † once, skip last sc; join with slip st to first sc: 176 ch-7 sps.
**Rnd 5:** Slip st in first 4 chs, ch 2, (dc, ch 5, work Cluster) in same ch, ch 3, sc in next ch-7 sp, (ch 7, sc in next ch-7 sp) twice, ch 3, ★ work (Cluster, ch 5, Cluster) in center ch of next ch-7, ch 3, sc in next ch-7 sp, (ch 7, sc in next ch-7 sp) twice, ch 3; repeat from ★ around; join with slip st to first dc: 44 Cluster groups.

Continued on page 94.

**Rnd 6:** Ch 2, dc in same st, ch 1, (dc, ch 1) 5 times in next ch-5 sp, work Cluster in next Cluster, ch 5, skip next ch-3 sp, sc in next ch-7 sp, ch 7, sc in next ch-7 sp, ch 5, ★ work Cluster in next Cluster, ch 1, (dc, ch 1) 5 times in next ch-5 sp, work Cluster in next Cluster, ch 5, skip next ch-3 sp, sc in next ch-7 sp, ch 7, sc in next ch-7 sp, ch 5; repeat from ★ around; join with slip st to first dc.

**Rnd 7:** Ch 2, dc in same st, ch 3, (dc in next dc, ch 3) 5 times, work Cluster in next Cluster, † ch 7, skip next ch-5 sp, sc in next ch-7 sp, ch 7, work Cluster in next Cluster, ch 3, (dc in next dc, ch 3) 5 times, work Cluster in next Cluster †, repeat from † to † 11 times **more**, ♥ ch 9, skip next ch-5 sp, dc in next ch-7 sp, work 3-Picot Group, ch 9, work Cluster in next Cluster, ch 3, (dc in next dc, ch 3) 5 times, work Cluster in next Cluster, repeat from † to † 8 times, ch 9, skip next ch-5 sp, dc in next ch-7 sp, work 3-Picot Group, ch 9 ♥, work Cluster in next Cluster, ch 3, (dc in next dc, ch 3) 5 times, work Cluster in next Cluster, repeat from † to † 12 times, then repeat from ♥ to ♥ once; join with slip st to first dc: 44 Fans.

**Rnd 8:** Ch 2, dc in same st, ch 5, (dc in next dc, ch 5) 5 times, work Cluster in next Cluster, † Tr tr in next sc, ch 7, in fifth ch from hook work (slip st, ch 6, slip st, ch 4, slip st), ch 2, Tr tr in same st as last Tr tr made, work Cluster in next Cluster, ch 5, (dc in next dc, ch 5) 5 times, work Cluster in next Cluster †, repeat from † to † 11 times **more**, ♥ ch 9, skip first Picot of next 3-Picot Group, (sc, ch 6, sc, ch 8, sc, ch 6, sc) in next Picot, ch 9, work Cluster in next Cluster, ch 5, (dc in next dc, ch 5) 5 times, work Cluster in next Cluster, repeat from † to † 8 times, ch 9, skip first Picot of next 3-Picot Group, (sc, ch 6, sc, ch 8, sc, ch 6, sc) in next Picot, ch 9 ♥, work Cluster in next Cluster, ch 5, (dc in next dc, ch 5) 5 times, work Cluster in next Cluster, repeat from † to † 12 times, then repeat from ♥ to ♥ once; join with slip st to first dc.

**Rnd 9:** Ch 1, sc in same st, (hdc, 3 dc, hdc) in next ch-5 sp, [sc in next dc, (hdc, 3 dc, hdc) in next ch-5 sp] 5 times, sc in next Cluster, † sc in next ch-4 sp, ch 7, (sc, ch 7, sc) in next ch-6 sp, ch 7, sc in next ch-4 sp, sc in next Cluster, (hdc, 3 dc, hdc) in next ch-5 sp, [sc in next dc, (hdc, 3 dc, hdc) in next ch-5 sp] 5 times, sc in next Cluster †, repeat from † to † 11 times **more**, ♥ ch 11, skip next 2 ch-sps, (sc, ch 7, sc, ch 9, sc, ch 7, sc) in next ch-8 sp, ch 11, sc in next Cluster, (hdc, 3 dc, hdc) in next ch-5 sp, [sc in next dc, (hdc, 3 dc, hdc) in next ch-5 sp] 5 times, sc in next Cluster, repeat from † to † 8 times, ch 11, skip next 2 ch-sps, (sc, ch 7, sc, ch 9, sc, ch 7, sc) in next ch-8 sp, ch 11 ♥, sc in next Cluster, (hdc, 3 dc, hdc) in next ch-5 sp, [sc in next dc, (hdc, 3 dc, hdc) in next ch-5 sp] 5 times, sc in next Cluster, repeat from † to † 12 times, then repeat from ♥ to ♥ once; join with slip st to first sc, finish off.

Make 4 tassels (**Figs. 27a & b, page 127**). Using photo as a guide, attach tassel to each corner.

Weave ribbon through Eyelet rnd and secure ends.

# NOSTALGIC RIPPLE

*Featuring fluffy puff stitches, this toasty warm afghan is a must for chasing away winter chills. The classic ripple pattern makes it perfect for any decor.*

**Finished Size:** 49" x 68"

## MATERIALS
Worsted Weight Yarn:
66 ounces, (1,870 grams, 3,190 yards)
Crochet hook, size I (5.50 mm) **or** size needed for gauge

**GAUGE:** Each repeat from point to point = 3³/4" and 10 rows = 4"

**Gauge Swatch:** 7¹/2"w x 4"h
Ch 35 **loosely.**
Work same as Afghan for 10 rows.
Finish off.

## STITCH GUIDE

**PUFF ST**
★ YO, insert hook in st indicated, YO and pull up a loop even with loop on hook; repeat from ★ 2 times **more**, YO and draw through all 7 loops on hook (**Fig. 15, page 122**).

**DC DECREASE** (uses next 2 sts)
★ YO, insert hook in **next** st, YO and pull up a loop, YO and draw through 2 loops on hook; repeat from ★ once **more**, YO and draw through all 3 loops on hook (**counts as one dc**).

**SC DECREASE** (uses next 2 dc)
Pull up a loop in next 2 dc, YO and draw through all 3 loops on hook (**counts as one sc**).

Ch 222 **loosely**.

**Row 1:** Dc in third ch from hook, (skip next ch, dc in next ch) twice, ch 1, (work Puff St in next ch, ch 1) 5 times, ★ dc in next ch, (skip next ch, dc in next ch) twice, skip next 2 chs, dc in next ch, (skip next ch, dc in next ch) twice, ch 1, (work Puff St in next ch, ch 1) 5 times; repeat from ★ across to last 6 chs, (dc in next ch, skip next ch) twice, dc decrease: 143 sts and 78 ch-1 sps.

**Row 2** (Right side)**:** Ch 1, turn; sc in first 3 dc, (sc in next ch-1 sp and in next Puff St) twice, 2 sc in next ch-1 sp, (sc in next Puff St and in next ch-1 sp) 3 times, ★ sc in next 2 dc, skip next dc, sc in next 3 dc, (sc in next ch-1 sp and in next Puff St) twice, 2 sc in next ch-1 sp, (sc in next Puff St and in next ch-1 sp) 3 times; repeat from ★ across to last 3 dc, sc in next dc, sc decrease: 221 sc.

**Note:** Loop a short piece of yarn around any stitch to mark Row 2 as **right** side.

**Row 3:** Ch 2, turn; dc in next sc, (skip next sc, dc in next sc) twice, ch 1, (work Puff St in next sc, ch 1) 5 times, ★ dc in next sc, (skip next sc, dc in next sc) twice, skip next 2 sc, dc in next sc, (skip next sc, dc in next sc) twice, ch 1, (work Puff St in next sc, ch 1) 5 times; repeat from ★ across to last 6 sc, (dc in next sc, skip next sc) twice, dc decrease.

Repeat Rows 2 and 3 until Afghan measures 68" from beginning ch.

Finish off.

Holding 8 strands of yarn together, add fringe in each point across short edges of Afghan **(Figs. 28a & c, page 127)**.

# BABY-SOFT WRAP

*Fashioned from soft baby sport weight yarn, this cuddly wrap is a sweet indulgence. The blissful blue and white afghan is embellished with pretty fringe.*

**Finished Size:** 35" x 44"

## MATERIALS
Baby Sport Weight Yarn:
    Blue - 18 ounces, (510 grams, 1,815 yards)
    White - 5 ounces, (140 grams, 505 yards)
Crochet hook, size G (4.00 mm) **or** size needed for gauge
Yarn needle

**GAUGE:** Each Square = 4³/₄"

## STITCH GUIDE

**LONG SINGLE CROCHET** *(abbreviated LSC)*
Working **around** slip st, insert hook in st or sp indicated, YO and pull up a loop even with last st made, YO and draw through both loops on hook *(Fig. 17, page 123)* **(counts as one sc)**.

## SQUARE (Make 63)
With Blue, ch 4; join with slip st to form a ring.
**Rnd 1 (Right side):** Ch 1, 8 sc in ring; join with slip st to first sc.
*Note:* Loop a short piece of yarn around any stitch to mark Rnd 1 as **right** side.
**Rnd 2:** Ch 3 **(counts as first dc, now and throughout)**, (2 dc, ch 1, 3 dc) in same st, slip st in next sc, ★ (3 dc, ch 1, 3 dc) in next sc, slip st in next sc; repeat from ★ 2 times **more**; join with slip st to first dc, finish off: 24 dc and 4 slip sts.
**Rnd 3:** With **right** side facing, join White with sc in any ch-1 sp *(see Joining With Sc, page 126)*; 2 sc in same sp, sc in next 3 dc, work LSC in sc on Rnd 1 **below** next slip st, sc in next 3 dc, ★ 3 sc in next ch-1 sp, sc in next 3 dc, work LSC in sc on Rnd 1 **below** next slip st, sc in next 3 dc; repeat from ★ 2 times **more**; join with slip st to first sc, finish off: 40 sc.
**Rnd 4:** With **right** side facing, join Blue with sc in center sc of any corner 3-sc group; ch 2, skip next 2 sc, sc in next sc, ch 2, skip next 3 sc, sc in next sc, ch 2, skip next 2 sc, ★ (sc, ch 2) twice in next sc, skip next 2 sc, sc in next sc, ch 2, skip next 3 sc, sc in next sc, ch 2, skip next 2 sc; repeat from ★ 2 times **more**, sc in same st as first sc, hdc in first sc to form last ch-2 sp: 16 ch-2 sps.

**Rnd 5:** Ch 3, (2 dc, ch 2, 3 dc) in same sp, slip st in next ch-2 sp, ★ (3 dc, ch 2, 3 dc) in next ch-2 sp, slip st in next ch-2 sp; repeat from ★ around; join with slip st to first dc, finish off: 48 dc and 8 ch-2 sps.
**Rnd 6:** With **right** side facing, join White with sc in any corner ch-2 sp; 2 sc in same sp, ★ † sc in next 3 dc, work LSC in ch-2 sp on Rnd 4 **below** next slip st, sc in next 3 dc, sc in next ch-2 sp and in next 3 dc, work LSC in ch-2 sp on Rnd 4 **below** next slip st, sc in next 3 dc †, 3 sc in next ch-2 sp; repeat from ★ 2 times **more**, then repeat from † to † once; join with slip st to first sc, finish off: 72 sc.
**Rnd 7:** With **right** side facing, join Blue with sc in center sc of any corner 3-sc group; ★ † ch 4, skip next 4 sc, hdc in next LSC, ch 2, skip next 3 sc, slip st in next sc, ch 2, skip next 3 sc, hdc in next LSC, ch 4, skip next 4 sc †, (sc, ch 2, sc) in next sc; repeat from ★ 2 times **more**, then repeat from † to † once, sc in same st as first sc, hdc in first sc to form last ch-2 sp: 20 sts and 20 sps.
**Rnd 8:** Ch 3, (2 dc, ch 2, 3 dc) in same sp, ★ † 4 dc in next ch-4 sp, dc in next hdc, (2 dc in next ch-2 sp, dc in next st) twice, 4 dc in next ch-4 sp †, (3 dc, ch 2, 3 dc) in next ch-2 sp; repeat from ★ 2 times **more**, then repeat from † to † once; join with slip st to first dc, finish off: 84 dc and 4 ch-2 sps.

## ASSEMBLY
Using Blue and working through both loops, whipstitch Squares together *(Fig. 26b, page 127)*, forming 7 vertical strips of 9 Squares each, beginning in second ch of first corner ch-2 and ending in first ch of next corner ch-2; whipstitch strips together in same manner.

## EDGING
With **right** side facing, join Blue with slip st in any corner ch-2 sp; ch 3, (2 dc, ch 2, 3 dc) in same sp, dc in each st and in each joining across to next corner ch-2 sp, ★ (3 dc, ch 2, 3 dc) in corner ch-2 sp, dc in each st and in each joining across to next corner ch-2 sp; repeat from ★ 2 times **more**; join with slip st to first dc, finish off.

Holding 2 strands of Blue together, add fringe evenly spaced across short edges of Afghan *(Figs. 28a & c, page 127)*.

# NINE-PATCH SPOOLS

*The seamstress will enjoy this whimsical creation! Carefully placed granny squares resemble old-fashioned sewing thread spools on this novel afghan.*

**Finished Size:** 49" x 67"

## MATERIALS
Worsted Weight Yarn:
- Black - 31 ounces, (880 grams, 1,950 yards)
- Brown - 6 ounces, (170 grams, 375 yards)
- Rose - 1 ounce, (30 grams, 65 yards)
- Green - 1 ounce, (30 grams, 65 yards)
- Lt Blue - 1 ounce, (30 grams, 65 yards)
- Blue - 1 ounce, (30 grams, 65 yards)
- Burgundy - 1 ounce, (30 grams, 65 yards)
- Purple - 1 ounce, (30 grams, 65 yards)
Crochet hook, size I (5.50 mm) **or** size needed for gauge
Yarn needle

**GAUGE:** Each Square = 3"

Referring to the Key, make the number of Squares specified in the colors indicated.

## SQUARE A
With color indicated, ch 4; join with slip st to form a ring.
**Rnd 1 (Right side):** Ch 3 **(counts as first dc, now and throughout)**, 2 dc in ring, ch 2, (3 dc in ring, ch 2) 3 times; join with slip st to first dc: 12 dc and 4 ch-2 sps.
*Note:* Loop a short piece of yarn around any stitch to mark Rnd 1 as **right** side.
**Rnd 2:** Slip st in next 2 dc and in next ch-2 sp, ch 3, (2 dc, ch 2, 3 dc) in same sp, ch 1, ★ (3 dc, ch 2, 3 dc) in next ch-2 sp, ch 1; repeat from ★ 2 times **more**; join with slip st to first dc, finish off: 24 dc and 8 sps.

## SQUARE B
With first color indicated, ch 4; join with slip st to form a ring.
**Rnd 1 (Right side):** Ch 5 **(counts as first dc plus ch 2)**, 3 dc in ring, cut first color, with second color, YO and draw through, ch 1, (3 dc, ch 2, 3 dc) in ring, cut second color, with first color, YO and draw through, ch 1, 2 dc in ring; join with slip st to first dc: 12 dc and 4 ch-2 sps.
*Note:* Mark Rnd 1 as **right** side.

**Rnd 2:** Slip st in first ch-2 sp, ch 3, (2 dc, ch 2, 3 dc) in same sp, ch 1, 3 dc in next ch-2 sp, cut first color, with second color, YO and draw through, ch 1, 3 dc in same sp, ch 1, (3 dc, ch 2, 3 dc) in next ch-2 sp, ch 1, 3 dc in next ch-2 sp, cut second color, with first color, YO and draw through, ch 1, 3 dc in same sp, ch 1; join with slip st to first dc, finish off: 24 dc and 8 sps.

## ASSEMBLY
With matching color, using Placement Diagram as a guide, and working through inside loops only, whipstitch Squares together **(Fig. 26a, page 127)**, forming 15 vertical strips of 21 Squares each, beginning in second ch of first corner and ending in first ch of next corner; whipstitch strips together in same manner.

### PLACEMENT DIAGRAM

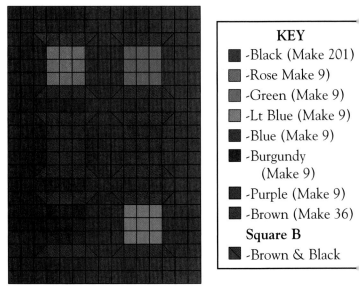

**KEY**
- ■ -Black (Make 201)
- ■ -Rose Make 9)
- ■ -Green (Make 9)
- ■ -Lt Blue (Make 9)
- ■ -Blue (Make 9)
- ■ -Burgundy (Make 9)
- ■ -Purple (Make 9)
- ■ -Brown (Make 36)
- **Square B**
- ■ -Brown & Black

## EDGING
**Rnd 1:** With **right** side facing, join Black with slip st in any corner ch-2 sp; ch 3, 2 dc in same sp, ★ † ch 1, skip next 3 dc, 3 dc in next ch-1 sp, ch 1, skip next 3 dc, [dc in next sp, dc in joining and in next sp, ch 1, skip next 3 dc, 3 dc in next ch-1 sp, ch 1, skip next 3 dc] across to next corner ch-2 sp †, (3 dc, ch 2, 3 dc) in corner ch-2 sp; repeat from ★ 2 times **more**, then repeat from † to † once, 3 dc in same sp as first dc, ch 1, sc in first dc to form last ch-2 sp: 444 dc and 148 sps.

**Rnd 2:** Ch 3, 2 dc in same sp, ch 1, (3 dc in next ch-1 sp, ch 1) across to next corner ch-2 sp, ★ (3 dc, ch 2, 3 dc) in corner ch-2 sp, ch 1, (3 dc in next ch-1 sp, ch 1) across to next corner ch-2 sp; repeat from ★ 2 times **more**, 3 dc in same sp as first dc, ch 1, sc in first dc to form last ch-2 sp: 456 dc and 152 sps.

**Rnd 3:** Ch 3, 2 dc in same sp, ch 1, (3 dc in next ch-1 sp, ch 1) across to next corner ch-2 sp, ★ (3 dc, ch 2, 3 dc) in corner ch-2 sp, ch 1, (3 dc in next ch-1 sp, ch 1) across to next corner ch-2 sp; repeat from ★ 2 times **more**, 3 dc in same sp as first dc, ch 2; join with slip st to first dc, finish off.

# RAMBLING ROSE

*This floral-inspired afghan will make a beautiful throw for the bed!*
*Two sizes of squares are combined to create this charming cover-up.*

**Finished Size:** 56" x 71"

**MATERIALS**
Worsted Weight Yarn:
Green - 34¹/2 ounces, (980 grams, 2,185 yards)
Off-White - 20 ounces, (570 grams, 1,265 yards)
Mauve - 11¹/2 ounces, (330 grams, 730 yards)
Crochet hook, size I (5.50 mm) **or** size needed for gauge
Yarn needle

**GAUGE:** Each Square A or B = 7¹/2"
Each Small Square = 3³/4"

**Gauge Swatch:** 2³/4"
Work same as Square A Rnds 1 and 2.

# SQUARE A (Make 32)
**Rnd 1 (Right side):** With Mauve, ch 4, 2 dc in fourth ch from hook, ch 3, (3 dc in same ch, ch 3) 3 times; join with slip st to top of beginning ch-4, finish off: 4 ch-3 sps.
*Note:* Loop a short piece of yarn around any stitch to mark Rnd 1 as **right** side.
**Rnd 2:** With **right** side facing, join Green with slip st in any ch-3 sp; ch 3 (**counts as first dc, now and throughout**), (2 dc, ch 3, 3 dc) in same sp, ch 1, ★ (3 dc, ch 3, 3 dc) in next ch-3 sp, ch 1; repeat from ★ 2 times **more**; join with slip st to first dc, finish off: 24 dc and 8 sps.
**Rnd 3:** With **right** side facing, join Off-White with sc in any ch-3 sp (*see Joining With Sc, page 126*); ch 5, sc in same sp, ch 5, sc in next ch-1 sp, ★ ch 5, (sc, ch 5) twice in next ch-3 sp, sc in next ch-1 sp; repeat from ★ 2 times **more**, ch 2, dc in first sc to form last ch-5 sp: 12 ch-5 sps.
**Rnd 4:** Ch 1, sc in same sp, ch 1, 9 dc in next ch-5 sp, ch 1, sc in next ch-5 sp, ★ ch 6, sc in next ch-5 sp, ch 1, 9 dc in next ch-5 sp, ch 1, sc in next ch-5 sp; repeat from ★ 2 times **more**, ch 2, tr in first sc to form last ch-6 sp: 36 dc and 4 ch-6 sps.
**Rnd 5:** Ch 1, sc in same sp, ★ † ch 3, skip next dc, dc in next dc, ch 3, skip next 2 dc, (dc, ch 5, dc) in next dc, ch 3, skip next 2 dc, dc in next dc, ch 3 †, sc in next ch-6 sp; repeat from ★ 2 times **more**, then repeat from † to † once; join with slip st to first sc: 20 sps.

**Rnd 6:** Slip st in first ch-3 sp, ch 3, 2 dc in same sp, ch 1, 3 dc in next ch-3 sp, ch 1, (3 dc, ch 3, 3 dc) in next ch-5 sp, ch 1, ★ (3 dc in next ch-3 sp, ch 1) 4 times, (3 dc, ch 3, 3 dc) in next ch-5 sp, ch 1; repeat from ★ 2 times **more**, (3 dc in next ch-3 sp, ch 1) twice; join with slip st to first dc, finish off: 72 dc and 24 sps.
**Rnd 7:** With **right** side facing, join Green with slip st in any corner ch-3 sp; ch 3, (2 dc, ch 3, 3 dc) in same sp, ch 1, (3 dc in next ch-1 sp, ch 1) 5 times, ★ (3 dc, ch 3, 3 dc) in next ch-3 sp, ch 1, (3 dc in next ch-1 sp, ch 1) 5 times; repeat from ★ 2 times **more**; join with slip st to first dc, finish off: 84 dc and 28 sps.

# SQUARE B (Make 31)
**SMALL SQUARE** (Make 124)
*Note:* Each Square B consists of 4 Small Squares.
**Rnd 1 (Right side):** With Off-White, ch 4, 2 dc in fourth ch from hook, ch 3, (3 dc in same ch, ch 3) 3 times; join with slip st to top of beginning ch-4, finish off: 4 ch-3 sps.
*Note:* Mark Rnd 1 as **right** side.
**Rnd 2:** With **right** side facing, join Mauve with slip st in any ch-3 sp; ch 3, (2 dc, ch 3, 3 dc) in same sp, ch 1, ★ (3 dc, ch 3, 3 dc) in next ch-3 sp, ch 1; repeat from ★ 2 times **more**; join with slip st to first dc, finish off: 24 dc and 8 sps.
**Rnd 3:** With **right** side facing, join Green with slip st in any ch-3 sp; ch 3, (2 dc, ch 3, 3 dc) in same sp, ch 1, 3 dc in next ch-1 sp, ch 1, ★ (3 dc, ch 3, 3 dc) in next ch-3 sp, ch 1, 3 dc in next ch-1 sp, ch 1; repeat from ★ 2 times **more**; join with slip st to first dc, finish off: 36 dc and 12 sps.

With Green and working through both loops, whipstitch Small Squares together (*Fig. 26b, page 127*), forming 2 vertical strips of 2 Small Squares each, beginning in center ch of first corner ch-3 and ending in center ch of next corner ch-3; whipstitch strips together in same manner.

# ASSEMBLY
With Green and using Placement Diagram, page 102, as a guide, whipstitch Squares A and B together, forming 7 vertical strips of 9 Squares each; whipstitch strips together in same manner.

# BORDER

**Rnd 1:** With **right** side facing, join Green with sc in top right corner ch-3 sp; ch 3, sc in same sp, † ch 1, skip next dc, sc in next dc, ch 1, (sc in next ch-1 sp, ch 1, skip next dc, sc in next dc, ch 1) 6 times, ♥ (sc in next sp, ch 1) twice, [skip next dc, sc in next dc, ch 1, (sc in next ch-1 sp, ch 1, skip next dc, sc in next dc, ch 1) twice, (sc in next sp, ch 1) twice] 2 times, skip next dc, sc in next dc, ch 1, (sc in next ch-1 sp, ch 1, skip next dc, sc in next dc, ch 1) 6 times ♥, repeat from ♥ to ♥ across to next corner ch-3 sp, (sc, ch 3, sc) in corner ch-3 sp, skip next dc, sc in next dc, ch 1, (sc in next ch-1 sp, ch 1, skip next dc, sc in next dc, ch 1) 6 times, repeat from ♥ to ♥ across to next corner ch-3 sp †, (sc, ch 3, sc) in corner ch-3 sp, repeat from † to † once; join with slip st to first sc: 464 sps.

Continued on page 102.

**Rnd 2:** Ch 1, (sc, ch 4) twice in first ch-3 sp, skip next ch-1 sp, (sc in next ch-1 sp, ch 4, skip next ch-1 sp) across to next corner ch-3 sp, ★ (sc, ch 4) twice in corner ch-3 sp, skip next ch-1 sp, (sc in next ch-1 sp, ch 4, skip next ch-1 sp) across to next corner ch-3 sp; repeat from ★ 2 times **more**; join with slip st to first sc: 236 ch-4 sps.

**Rnd 3:** Ch 1, (sc, ch 4) twice in first ch-4 sp, (sc in next ch-4 sp, ch 4) across to next corner ch-4 sp, ★ (sc, ch 4) twice in corner ch-4 sp, (sc in next ch-4 sp, ch 4) across to next corner ch-4 sp; repeat from ★ 2 times **more**; join with slip st to first sc: 240 ch-4 sps.

**Rnd 4:** Ch 1, (sc, ch 5) twice in first ch-4 sp, ★ (sc in next ch-4 sp, ch 5) across to next corner ch-4 sp, (sc, ch 5) twice in corner ch-4 sp; repeat from ★ 2 times **more**, sc in next ch-4 sp, (ch 5, sc in next ch-4 sp) across, ch 2, dc in first sc to form last ch-5 sp: 244 ch-5 sps.

**Rnd 5:** Ch 1, sc in same sp, 9 dc in next ch-5 sp, ★ sc in next ch-5 sp, (7 dc in next ch-5 sp, sc in next ch-5 sp) across to next corner ch-5 sp, 9 dc in corner ch-5 sp; repeat from ★ 2 times **more**, (sc in next ch-5 sp, 7 dc in next ch-5 sp) across; join with slip st to first sc, finish off.

## PLACEMENT DIAGRAM

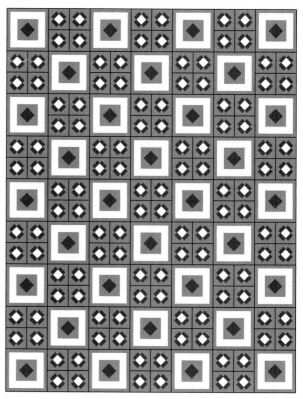

# WINTRY FANS

*Wrap yourself in comfort with this plush cover-up worked holding two strands of yarn together. The two-tone afghan is finished with plentiful fringe.*

**Finished Size:** 49" x 66"  73y

## MATERIALS
Worsted Weight Yarn:
    Lavender - 37 ounces, (1,050 grams, 2,430 yards)
    Ecru - 36 ounces, (1,020 grams, 2,365 yards)
    Crochet hook, size Q (15.00 mm)

**Note:** Each row is worked across length of Afghan holding two strands of yarn together.

**GAUGE:** In pattern, (sc, 2 dc) 6 times = 11"
        and 7 rows = 6½"

**Gauge Swatch:** 7¾"w x 6½"h
Ch 15 **loosely.**
Work same as Afghan for 7 rows.
Finish off.

## COLOR SEQUENCE
One row **each:** Lavender *(Fig. 23a, page 126)*, (Ecru, Lavender) throughout.

With Lavender, ch 111 **loosely.**
**Row 1** (Right side)**:** 2 Dc in third ch from hook, ★ skip next 2 chs, (sc, 2 dc) in next ch; repeat from ★ across to last 3 chs, skip next 2 chs, sc in last ch: 36 sc.
**Note:** Loop a short piece of yarn around any stitch to mark Row 1 as **right** side.
**Row 2:** Ch 2, turn; 2 dc in first sc, ★ skip next 2 dc, (sc, 2 dc) in next sc; repeat from ★ across to last 3 sts, skip next 2 dc, sc in top of beginning ch.
**Row 3:** Ch 2, turn; 2 dc in first sc, ★ skip next 2 dc, (sc, 2 dc) in next sc; repeat from ★ across to last 3 sts, skip next 2 dc, sc in top of turning ch.
Repeat Row 3 until Afghan measures 49" from beginning ch, ending by working one row Lavender; finish off.

Holding 8 strands of corresponding color together, add fringe evenly across short edges of Afghan *(Figs. 28b & d, page 127)*.

# HOME
## for the holidays

There's nothing like being home for the holidays, because celebrations are always more memorable when shared with family and friends. Inspired by the wonderful occasions we take pleasure in all through the year, this fun collection includes afghans that everyone will enjoy. The easy-to-create patterns range from fabulous ripples to stunning granny squares.

# SWEETHEART PLAID

*Surprise your valentine with this sweetheart of an afghan. Because of the plush wrap's pretty pattern and luxurious fringe, it'll be love at first sight!*

**Finished Size:** 47" x 62"

## MATERIALS
Worsted Weight Yarn:
Red - 33 ounces, (940 grams, 2,150 yards)
White - 18 ounces, (510 grams, 1,175 yards)
Crochet hook, size I (5.50 mm) **or** size needed for gauge
Yarn needle

**GAUGE:** Each Square = 5"

**Gauge Swatch:** 3¹/₂"
Work same as Square Rnds 1-3.

## STITCH GUIDE

> **FRONT POST TREBLE CROCHET**
> *(abbreviated FPtr)*
> YO twice, insert hook from **front** to **back** around post of st indicated, YO and pull up a loop *(Fig. 12, page 122)*, (YO and draw through 2 loops on hook) 3 times. Skip st behind FPtr.

## SQUARE (Make 108)
**Rnd 1 (Right side):** With Red, ch 4, 2 dc in fourth ch from hook **(3 skipped chs count as first dc)**, ch 1, (3 dc in same ch, ch 1) 3 times; join with slip st to first dc: 12 dc and 4 ch-1 sps.
*Note:* Loop a short piece of yarn around any stitch to mark Rnd 1 as **right** side.
**Rnd 2:** Ch 3 **(counts as first dc, now and throughout)**, dc in next 2 dc, (dc, ch 1, dc) in next ch-1 sp, ★ dc in next 3 dc, (dc, ch 1, dc) in next ch-1 sp; repeat from ★ 2 times **more**; join with slip st to first dc, finish off: 20 dc and 4 ch-1 sps.
**Rnd 3:** With **right** side facing, join White with sc in any ch-1 sp *(see Joining With Sc, page 126)*; sc in same sp and in next 5 dc, ★ 3 sc in next ch-1 sp, sc in next 5 sc; repeat from ★ 2 times **more**, sc in same sp as first sc; join with slip st to first sc, finish off: 32 sc.
**Rnd 4:** With **right** side facing, join Red with slip st in same st as joining; ch 3, dc in same st and in next 7 sc, ★ 3 dc in next sc, dc in next 7 sc; repeat from ★ 2 times **more**, dc in same st as first dc; join with slip st to first dc, finish off: 40 dc.

**Rnd 5:** With **right** side facing, join White with sc in second dc to right of joining; ★ † work FPtr around sc one rnd **below** next dc, 3 sc in next dc, work FPtr around **same** st as last FPtr made †, sc in next 7 dc; repeat from ★ 2 times **more**, then repeat from † to † once, sc in last 6 dc; join with slip st to first sc, finish off: 48 sts.

## ASSEMBLY
Using White and working through both loops, whipstitch Squares together *(Fig. 26b, page 127)*, forming 9 vertical strips of 12 Squares each, beginning in center sc of first corner and ending in center sc of next corner; whipstitch strips together in same manner.

## EDGING
**Rnd 1:** With **right** side facing, join Red with slip st in center sc of any corner 3-sc group; ch 3, 2 dc in same st, ★ † dc in next sc, ch 1, skip next FPtr, dc in next 7 sc, ch 1, skip next FPtr, dc in next sc, (dc in same st as joining on same Square, ch 1, dc in same st as joining on next Square and in next sc, ch 1, skip next FPtr, dc in next 7 sc, ch 1, skip next FPtr, dc in next sc) across to center sc of next corner 3-sc group †, 3 dc in center sc; repeat from ★ 2 times **more**, then repeat from † to † once; join with slip st to first dc, finish off: 466 dc and 122 ch-1 sps.
**Rnd 2:** With **right** side facing, join White with sc in center dc of any 3-dc group; 2 sc in same st, sc in next 2 dc, ★ † working in **front** of next ch-1, work FPtr around next FPtr on Rnd 5 of Square, sc in next 7 dc, working in **front** of next ch-1, work FPtr around next FPtr on Rnd 5 of Square, sc in next 2 dc, (working in **front** of next ch-1, tr in next joining, sc in next 2 dc, working in **front** of next ch-1, work FPtr around next FPtr on Rnd 5 of Square, sc in next 7 dc, working in **front** of next ch-1, work FPtr around next FPtr on Rnd 5 of Square, sc in next 2 dc) across to center dc of next 3-dc group †, 3 sc in center dc; repeat from ★ 2 times **more**, then repeat from † to † once; join with slip st to first sc, finish off: 596 sts.
**Rnd 3:** With **right** side facing, join Red with sc in any st; sc in each st around working 3 sc in center sc of each 3-sc group; join with slip st to first sc, finish off.

Holding five strands of Red together, add fringe evenly across short edges of Afghan *(Figs. 28a & c, page 127)*.

# SHAMROCK RIPPLE

*Rolling ripples created from emerald cluster stitches resemble a windswept field of clover on this classic Irish charmer. The St. Patrick's Day-inspired afghan is just right for quiet daydreaming.*

**Finished Size:** 48" x 69"

## MATERIALS
Worsted Weight Yarn:
  Green - 24 ounces, (680 grams, 1,645 yards)
  Lt Green - 15 ounces, (430 grams, 1,030 yards)
  Dk Green - 8 ounces, (230 grams, 550 yards)
Crochet hook, size I (5.50 mm) **or** size needed for gauge

**GAUGE:** 2 repeats from point to point = 5" and
        8 rows = 3¹/2"

**Gauge Swatch:** 5¹/2"w x 3¹/2"h
Ch 22 **loosely.**
Work same as Afghan for 8 rows.
Finish off.

## STITCH GUIDE

**DECREASE** (uses next 3 sc)
YO, insert hook in **next** sc, YO and pull up a loop, YO and draw through 2 loops on hook, YO twice, insert hook in **next** sc, YO and pull up a loop, (YO and draw through 2 loops on hook) twice, YO, insert hook in **next** sc, YO and pull up a loop, YO and draw through 2 loops on hook, YO and draw through all 4 loops on hook.
**2-DC CLUSTER**
★ YO, insert hook in sc indicated, YO and pull up a loop, YO and draw through 2 loops on hook; repeat from ★ once **more,** YO and draw through all 3 loops on hook (*Figs. 16a & b, page 123*).
**4-DC CLUSTER**
★ YO, insert hook in tr indicated, YO and pull up a loop, YO and draw through 2 loops on hook; repeat from ★ 3 times **more,** YO and draw through all 5 loops on hook. Push Cluster to **right** side.

With Green, ch 192 **loosely.**
**Row 1:** Sc in second ch from hook, ch 1, skip next ch, sc in next ch, ch 1, ★ † skip next 2 chs, (dc, ch 2, dc) in next ch, ch 1, skip next 2 chs, sc in next ch, ch 1 †, (skip next ch, sc in next ch, ch 1) twice; repeat from ★ across to last 8 chs, then repeat from † to † once, skip next ch, sc in last ch: 95 sps.
**Row 2** (Right side): Ch 1, turn; sc in first sc and in next ch-1 sp, ch 1, ★ † skip next sc, dc in next dc, ch 1, (dc, ch 1) 3 times in next ch-2 sp, dc in next dc, ch 1 †, skip next ch-1 sp, (sc in next ch-1 sp, ch 1) twice; repeat from ★ 17

times **more,** then repeat from † to † once, skip next ch-1 sp, sc in next ch-1 sp and in last sc; finish off: 132 ch-1 sps.
*Note:* Loop a short piece of yarn around any stitch to mark Row 2 as **right** side.
**Row 3:** With **wrong** side facing, join Dk Green with sc in first sc (*see Joining with Sc, page 126*); ch 1, skip next sc, (sc in next dc, ch 1) 5 times, ★ skip next ch-1 sp, sc in next ch-1 sp, ch 1, skip next sc, (sc in next dc, ch 1) 5 times; repeat from ★ across to last 2 sc, skip next sc, sc in last sc; finish off: 114 ch-1 sps.
**Row 4:** With **right** side facing, join Lt Green with slip st in first sc; ch 2, (dc in next sc, ch 1) twice, (dc, ch 3, dc) in next sc, ch 1, dc in next sc, ch 1, ★ decrease, ch 1, dc in next sc, ch 1, (dc, ch 3, dc) in next sc, ch 1, dc in next sc, ch 1; repeat from ★ across to last 2 sc, (YO, insert hook in next sc, YO and pull up a loop, YO and draw through 2 loops on hook) twice, YO and draw through all 3 loops on hook; finish off: 95 sps.
**Row 5:** With **wrong** side facing, join Green with sc in first st; ch 1, (sc in next dc, ch 1) twice, sc in next ch-3 sp, ch 1, sc in next dc, ★ ch 1, (skip next ch-1 sp, sc in next st, ch 1) 4 times, sc in next ch-3 sp, ch 1, sc in next dc; repeat from ★ across to last 2 ch-1 sps, (ch 1, sc in next dc) twice; finish off: 114 ch-1 sps.
**Row 6:** Repeat Row 4.
**Row 7:** With Dk Green, repeat Row 5.
**Row 8:** With **right** side facing, join Green with slip st in first sc; ch 3, work 2-dc Cluster in next sc, ch 1, hdc in next sc, ch 1, sc in next sc, ch 1, hdc in next sc, ch 1, work 2-dc Cluster in next sc, ★ tr in next sc, work 2-dc Cluster in next sc, ch 1, hdc in next sc, ch 1, sc in next sc, ch 1, hdc in next sc, ch 1, work 2-dc Cluster in next sc; repeat from ★ across to last sc, dc in last sc: 76 ch-1 sps.
**Row 9:** Ch 1, turn; sc in first 2 sts and in next ch-1 sp, ch 1, skip next hdc, (dc, ch 2, dc) in next sc, ch 1, ★ skip next ch-1 sp, sc in next ch-1 sp and in next 2-dc Cluster, work 4-dc Cluster in next tr, sc in next 2-dc Cluster and in next ch-1 sp, ch 1, skip next hdc, (dc, ch 2, dc) in next sc, ch 1; repeat from ★ across to last 2 ch-1 sps, skip next ch-1 sp, sc in next ch-1 sp and in last 2 sts: 57 sps.
**Row 10:** Ch 1, turn; sc in first 2 sc, ch 1, skip next sc, dc in next dc, ch 1, (dc, ch 1) 3 times in next ch-2 sp, dc in next dc, ch 1, ★ skip next sc, sc in next 3 sts, ch 1, skip next sc, dc in next dc, ch 1, (dc, ch 1) 3 times in next ch-2 sp, dc in next dc, ch 1; repeat from ★ across to last 3 sc, skip next sc, sc in last 2 sc; finish off: 114 ch-1 sps.

**Row 11:** With **wrong** side facing, join Dk Green with sc in first sc; ch 1, skip next sc, (sc in next dc, ch 1) 5 times, ★ skip next sc, sc in next sc, ch 1, skip next sc, (sc in next dc, ch 1) 5 times; repeat from ★ across to last 2 sc, skip next sc, sc in last sc; finish off.

Repeat Rows 4-11 until Afghan measures 67" from beginning ch, ending by working Row 8.

**Last Row:** Ch 1, turn; sc in first dc, ch 1, (sc in next ch-1 sp, ch 1) 4 times, ★ skip next 2-dc Cluster, sc in next tr, ch 1, (sc in next ch-1 sp, ch 1) 4 times; repeat from ★ across to last 2 sts, skip next 2-dc Cluster, sc in top of turning ch; do **not** finish off.

# EDGING

**Rnd 1:** Ch 1, turn; (sc, ch 2, sc) in first sc, ch 1, (sc in next sc, ch 1) across to last sc, (sc, ch 2, sc) in last sc, ch 1; working in end of rows, skip first row, (sc in next row, ch 1) 6 times, † skip next row, (sc in next row, ch 1) 7 times †, repeat from † to † across to last 2 rows, skip last 2 rows; working in free loops of beginning ch *(Fig. 25b, page 126)*, (sc, ch 2, sc) in ch at base of first sc, ch 1, (skip next ch, sc in next ch, ch 1) across to last 2 chs, skip next ch, (sc, ch 2, sc) in last ch, ch 1; working in end of rows, skip first 2 rows, (sc in next row, ch 1) 7 times, repeat from † to † across to last 8 rows, skip next row, (sc in next row, ch 1) 6 times, skip last row; join with slip st to first sc.

**Rnd 2:** Do **not** turn; ch 1, (slip st, ch 1) twice in first ch-2 sp, ★ (slip st in next ch-1 sp, ch 1) across to next ch-2 sp, (slip st, ch 1) twice in ch-2 sp; repeat from ★ 2 times **more**, (slip st in next ch-1 sp, ch 1) across; join with slip st to st at base of first ch-1; finish off.

# EASTER GRANNY

*Celebrate the arrival of spring with this blanket of pretty pastel flowers. The Eastertime afghan is ideal for snuggling up with your favorite little "bunnies." Simple strips of granny squares are easily whipstitched together for a quick finish.*

**Finished Size:** 51" x 71"

## MATERIALS
Worsted Weight Yarn:
  White - 19 ounces, (540 grams, 1,250 yards)
  Pink - 15 ounces, (430 grams, 985 yards)
  Blue - 15 ounces, (430 grams, 985 yards)
  Green - 8 ounces, (230 grams, 525 yards)
Crochet hook, size H (5.00 mm) **or** size needed for gauge
Yarn needle

**GAUGE:** Each Square = 4$^{1}/4$"

## STITCH GUIDE

> **LONG DOUBLE CROCHET** *(abbreviated LDC)*
> YO, insert hook in st indicated, YO and pull up a loop even with Row 1, (YO and draw through 2 loops on hook) twice *(Fig. 17, page 123)*.

# STRIP A
## SQUARE A (Make 80)
With Pink, ch 3; join with slip st to form a ring.
**Rnd 1 (Right side):** Ch 3 **(counts as first dc, now and throughout)**, 2 dc in ring, ch 2, (3 dc in ring, ch 2) 3 times; join with slip st to first dc, finish off: 12 dc.
*Note:* Loop a short piece of yarn around any stitch to mark Rnd 1 as **right** side.
**Rnd 2:** With **right** side facing, join White with slip st in any ch-2 sp; ch 3, (2 dc, ch 2, 3 dc) in same sp, ch 1, ★ (3 dc, ch 2, 3 dc) in next ch-2 sp, ch 1; repeat from ★ around; join with slip st to first dc, finish off: 24 dc.
**Rnd 3:** With **right** side facing, join Green with slip st in any corner ch-2 sp; ch 3, (2 dc, ch 2, 3 dc) in same sp, ch 1, 3 dc in next ch-1 sp, ch 1, ★ (3 dc, ch 2, 3 dc) in next corner ch-2 sp, ch 1, 3 dc in next ch-1 sp, ch 1; repeat from ★ around; join with slip st to first dc, finish off: 36 dc.
**Rnd 4:** With **right** side facing, join Blue with slip st in any corner ch-2 sp; ch 3, (2 dc, ch 2, 3 dc) in same sp, ch 1, (3 dc in next ch-1 sp, ch 1) twice, ★ (3 dc, ch 2, 3 dc) in next corner ch-2 sp, ch 1, (3 dc in next ch-1 sp, ch 1) twice; repeat from ★ around; join with slip st to first dc, finish off: 48 dc.

## SQUARE ASSEMBLY
Using Blue and working through both loops, whipstitch Squares together *(Fig. 26b, page 127)*, forming 5 vertical Strips of 16 Squares each, beginning in second ch of first corner ch-2 and ending in first ch of next corner ch-2.

## INSIDE BORDER
**Row 1:** With **right** side facing and working across long edge, join White with slip st in corner ch-2 sp of any Strip; ch 3, 2 dc in same sp, ch 1, (3 dc in next ch-1 sp, ch 1) 3 times, ★ (3 dc in next ch-2 sp at joining, ch 1) twice, (3 dc in next ch-1 sp, ch 1) 3 times; repeat from ★ across to next corner ch-2 sp, 3 dc in corner ch-2 sp; finish off: 240 dc.
**Row 2:** With **right** side facing, join Pink with slip st in first dc; ch 1, sc in same st, skip next dc, sc in next dc, † working around next ch-1, work LDC in center dc of next 3-dc group on Rnd 4 of Square, skip next dc on Row 1, sc in next 2 dc †, repeat from † to † 3 times **more**, ★ working around next ch-1, work LDC in next joining, skip next dc, sc in next 2 dc, repeat from † to † 4 times; repeat from ★ across; finish off: 79 LDC.
Work Inside Border across both long edges of 3 Strips (inner Strips) and across only one long edge of 2 Strips (outer Strips).

# STRIP B
## SQUARE B (Make 64)
Work same as Square A in the following color sequence: 1 Rnd each of Green, White, Pink, and Blue.

## SQUARE ASSEMBLY
Work same as Strip A, forming 4 vertical Strips of 16 Squares each.

## INSIDE BORDER
Work same as Strip A, working across both long edges of all 4 Strips.

# STRIP ASSEMBLY
With Pink and working through both loops across Inside Border, whipstitch Strips together, alternating Strip A and Strip B, and placing an outer Strip A on each end.

# EDGING

**Rnd 1:** With **right** side facing, join White with slip st in top right corner ch-2 sp; ch 3, (2 dc, ch 2, 3 dc) in same sp, ch 1, (3 dc in next ch-1 sp, ch 1) 3 times, † 3 dc in next ch-2 sp (same sp as Inside Border), ch 1, 3 dc in joining, ch 1, 3 dc in next ch-2 sp (same sp as Inside Border), (3 dc in next ch-1 sp, ch 1) 3 times †, repeat from † to † across to next corner ch-2 sp, (3 dc, ch 2, 3 dc) in corner ch-2 sp, ch 1, (3 dc in next ch-1 sp, ch 1) across to next corner ch-2 sp, (3 dc, ch 2, 3 dc) in corner ch-2 sp, ch 1, (3 dc in next ch-1 sp, ch 1) 3 times, repeat from † to † across to next corner ch-2 sp, (3 dc, ch 2, 3 dc) in corner ch-2 sp, ch 1, (3 dc in next ch-1 sp, ch 1) across; join with slip st to first dc, finish off.

**Rnd 2:** With **wrong** side facing, join Pink with slip st in any corner ch-2 sp; ch 3, (2 dc, ch 2, 3 dc) in same sp, ch 1, (3 dc in next ch-1 sp, ch 1) across to next corner ch-2 sp, ★ (3 dc, ch 2, 3 dc) in corner ch-2 sp, ch 1, (3 dc in next ch-1 sp, ch 1) across to next corner ch-2 sp; repeat from ★ around; join with slip st to first dc, finish off.

**Rnd 3:** With **right** side facing and White, repeat Rnd 2.

111

# AMERICAN FIREWORKS

*Star-spangled blocks explode in radiant red, white, and blue on this spirited wrap. You'll be proud to display the all-American afghan — a salute to our great country — on the Fourth of July and other patriotic holidays throughout the year.*

**Finished Size:** 56" x 66"

## MATERIALS
Worsted Weight Yarn:
Ecru - 11½ ounces, (330 grams, 725 yards)
Red - 20 ounces, (570 grams, 1,260 yards)
Blue- 24 ounces, (680 grams, 1,510 yards)
Crochet hook, size J (6.00 mm) **or** size needed for gauge
Yarn needle

**GAUGE:** Each Square = 5"

**Gauge Swatch:** 3¼"
Work same as Square Rnds 1 and 2.

## STITCH GUIDE

**BEGINNING CLUSTER**
Ch 2, ★ YO, insert hook in **same** sp, YO and pull up a loop, YO and draw through 2 loops on hook; repeat from ★ once **more**, YO and draw through all 3 loops on hook (*Figs. 16a & b, page 123*).
**CLUSTER**
★ YO, insert hook in sp indicated, YO and pull up a loop, YO and draw through 2 loops on hook; repeat from ★ 2 times **more**, YO and draw through all 4 loops on hook.

## SQUARE
Make 143 in the following color sequences:

|  | Square A | Square B |
|---|---|---|
| Make | 72 | 71 |
| Rnd 1 | Ecru | Ecru |
| Rnd 2 | Red | Blue |
| Rnd 3 | Ecru | Ecru |
| Rnds 4 and 5 | Blue | Red |

With Ecru, ch 4; join with slip st to form a ring.
**Rnd 1 (Right side):** Ch 4, (dc in ring, ch 1) 11 times; join with slip st to third ch of beginning ch-4, finish off: 12 ch-1 sps.
*Note:* Loop a short piece of yarn around any stitch to mark Rnd 1 as **right** side.
**Rnd 2:** With **right** side facing, join next color with slip st in any ch-1 sp; work beginning Cluster, ch 3, (work Cluster

in next ch-1 sp, ch 3) around; join with slip st to top of beginning Cluster, finish off.
**Rnd 3:** With **right** side facing, join Ecru with slip st in any ch-3 sp; ch 1, sc in same sp, ch 5, (sc in next ch-3 sp, ch 5) around; join with slip st to first sc, finish off.
**Rnd 4:** With **right** side facing, join next color with slip st in any ch-5 sp; ch 1, sc in same sp, ★ † ch 1, (5 dc, ch 1) twice in next ch-5 sp, sc in next ch-5 sp, ch 3 †, sc in next ch-5 sp; repeat from ★ 2 times **more**, then repeat from † to † once; join with slip st to first sc: 48 sts and 16 sps.
**Rnd 5:** Ch 1, sc in same st and in next ch-1 sp, ★ † sc in next 5 dc, 3 sc in next ch-1 sp, sc in next 5 dc, sc in next ch-1 sp and in next sc, 3 sc in next ch-3 sp †, sc in next sc and in next ch-1 sp; repeat from ★ 2 times **more**, then repeat from † to † once; join with slip st to first sc, finish off: 80 sc.

## ASSEMBLY
Afghan is assembled by weaving Squares together to form strips as follows:
Place two Squares side by side on a flat surface. Beginning in center sc of first corner, sew through both Squares once to secure the beginning of the seam, leaving an ample yarn end to weave in later. Insert needle from **right** to **left** through back strand (just below top loop) of first st on both pieces (*Fig. 1a*). Bring the needle around and insert it from **right** to **left** through the next strand on both pieces; repeat along the edge, ending in center sc of next corner.

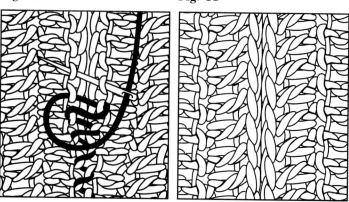

| **Fig. 1a** | **Fig. 1b** |
|---|---|
| wrong side | right side |

Using Blue and alternating Squares A and B throughout, weave 13 Squares together, forming 11 vertical strips, beginning and ending 6 strips with Square A and beginning and ending 5 strips with Square B; weave strips together in same manner.

## EDGING

**Rnd 1:** With **wrong** side facing, join Blue with slip st in any sc; ch 1, sc evenly around working 3 sc in center sc of each corner; join with slip st to first sc.

**Rnd 2:** Ch 1, turn; sc in each sc around working 3 sc in center sc of each corner; join with slip st to first sc, finish off.

# BEWITCHING HALLOWEEN WRAP

*Chase away those goose bumps with our bewitching Halloween wrap! Striking silhouettes of black cats are formed with the simple placement of one- and two-color granny squares. Gold borders surround the dramatic blocks.*

**Finished Size:** 48" x 73"

## MATERIALS
Worsted Weight Yarn:
Gold - 15 ounces, (430 grams, 945 yards)
Black - 26 ounces, (740 grams, 1,635 yards)
Cream - 10 ounces, (280 grams, 630 yards)
Crochet hook, size J (6.00 mm) **or** size needed for gauge
Yarn needle

**GAUGE:** Each Square = 2¹/2"

Referring to the Key, make the number of squares specified in the colors indicated.

## SQUARE A
With color indicated ch 4; join with slip st to form a ring.
**Rnd 1 (Right side):** Ch 3, 15 dc in ring; join with slip st to top of beginning ch: 16 sts.
**Note:** Loop a short piece of yarn around any stitch to mark Rnd 1 as **right** side.
**Rnd 2:** Ch 5 **(counts as first tr plus ch 1, now and throughout)**, dc in same st, ★ dc in next 3 dc, (dc, ch 1, tr, ch 1, dc) in next dc; repeat from ★ 2 times **more**, dc in last 3 dc and in same st as joining, ch 1; join with slip st to first tr, finish off: 24 sts.

## SQUARE B
With Cream, ch 4; join with slip st to form a ring.
**Rnd 1 (Right side):** Ch 3, 7 dc in ring changing to Black in last dc worked, cut Cream, 8 dc in ring; with Cream join with slip st to top of beginning ch **(Fig. 23b, page 126)**, cut Black: 16 sts.
**Note:** Mark Rnd 1 as **right** side.
**Rnd 2:** Ch 5, dc in same st and in next 3 dc, (dc, ch 1, tr, ch 1, dc) in next dc, dc in next 4 dc, cut Cream, with Black, ch 1, (tr, ch 1, dc) in same st, dc in next 3 dc, (dc, ch 1, tr, ch 1, dc) in next dc, dc in last 3 dc and in same st as joining, ch 1; join with slip st to first tr, finish off: 24 sts.

## ASSEMBLY
With matching color, using Diagram A as a guide, and working through inside loops only, whipstitch Squares together **(Fig. 26a, page 127)**, forming 13 vertical strips of 23 Squares each, beginning in first corner tr and ending in next corner tr; whipstitch strips together in same manner.

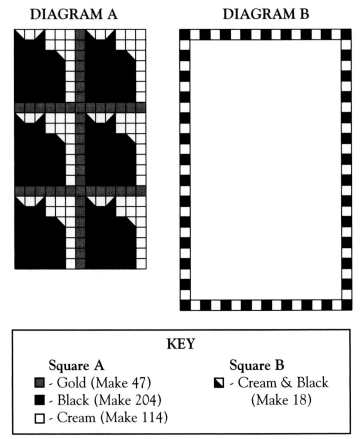

**DIAGRAM A**                    **DIAGRAM B**

| KEY | |
|---|---|
| **Square A** | **Square B** |
| ■ - Gold (Make 47) | ◨ - Cream & Black |
| ■ - Black (Make 204) | (Make 18) |
| □ - Cream (Make 114) | |

## BORDER
**Rnd 1:** With **right** side facing and working in Back Loops Only **(Fig. 24, page 126)**, join Gold with slip st in any corner tr; ch 5, dc in same st, ★ † dc in next ch-1 sp, dc in next 5 dc and in next ch-1 sp, (dc in next joining and in next ch-1 sp, dc in next 5 dc and in next ch-1 sp) across to next corner tr †, (dc, ch 1, tr, ch 1, dc) in corner tr; repeat from ★ 2 times **more**, then repeat from † to † once, dc in same st as joining, ch 1; join with slip st to first tr: 584 sts.

**Rnds 2-4:** Ch 5, working in both loops, dc in same st, dc in next ch-1 sp and in each dc across to next ch-1 sp, dc in next ch-1 sp, ★ (dc, ch 1, tr, ch 1, dc) in corner tr, dc in next ch-1 sp and in each dc across to next ch-1 sp, dc in next ch-1 sp; repeat from ★ around, dc in same st as joining, ch 1; join with slip st to first tr: 632 sts. Finish off.

Following Placement Diagram B, page 114, whipstitch remaining Squares together.
Whipstitch Squares to Border.

## EDGING
Work same as Rnds 1-4 of Border; finish off.

# YULETIDE THROW

*Like the treasured ornaments that you display year after year,
this Yuletide afghan will become a family heirloom. You'll want to
keep the eye-catching creation on hand all season long!*

**Finished Size:** 49" x 72"

## MATERIALS
Worsted Weight Yarn:
Dk Green - 25 ounces, (710 grams, 1,575 yards)
Green - 15 ounces, (430 grams, 945 yards)
Beige - 8 ounces, (230 grams, 505 yards)
Maroon - 8 ounces, (230 grams, 505 yards)
Crochet hook, size H (5.00 mm) **or** size needed for gauge

**GAUGE:** Each repeat from point to point = 3¹/4" and
8 rows = 5¹/2"

**Gauge Swatch:** 7"w x 5¹/2"h
Ch 40 **loosely.**
Work Rows 1-8 of Afghan.
Finish off.

## STITCH GUIDE

> **SHELL**
> (2 Dc, ch 2, 2 dc) in st or sp indicated.
> **LONG DOUBLE CROCHET** *(abbreviated LDC)*
> Working **around** ch-2 of previous row, insert hook in st
> or sp indicated in row **below** ch-2, YO and pull up a
> loop even with loop on hook, (YO and draw through
> 2 loops on hook) twice **(Fig. 17, page 123)**.

With Dk Green, ch 287 **loosely.**
**Row 1 (Right side):** Dc in fourth ch from hook **(3 skipped
chs count as first dc)**, ch 2, skip next 3 chs, 2 dc in next
ch, ch 2, skip next 3 chs, work Shell in next ch, ★ (ch 2,
skip next 3 chs, 2 dc in next ch) twice, skip next 2 chs,
(2 dc in next ch, ch 2, skip next 3 chs) twice, work Shell
in next ch; repeat from ★ across to last 9 chs, ch 2, skip
next 3 chs, 2 dc in next ch, ch 2, skip next 3 chs, dc in
last 2 chs: 15 Shells.
**Note:** Loop a short piece of yarn around any stitch to mark
Row 1 as **right** side.

**Row 2:** Ch 3 **(counts as first dc, now and throughout)**,
turn; working in beginning ch, LDC in center ch of next
3 skipped chs, ch 2, 2 LDC in center ch of next 3 skipped
chs, ch 2, work Shell in next Shell (ch-2 sp), ★ (ch 2,
2 LDC in center ch of next 3 skipped chs) twice, skip
next 4 dc, (2 LDC in center ch of next 3 skipped chs, ch 2)
twice, work Shell in next Shell; repeat from ★ across to
last 6 dc, ch 2, 2 LDC in center ch of next 3 skipped chs,
ch 2, LDC in center ch of next 3 skipped chs, skip next dc,
dc in last dc.
**Row 3:** Ch 3, turn; LDC in sp **between** 2 sts **below** first
ch-2 **(Fig. 20, page 124)**, ch 2, 2 LDC in sp **between** 2 dc
**below** next ch-2 (first half of Shell), ch 2, work Shell in
next Shell, ★ ch 2, 2 LDC in sp **between** 2 dc **below** next
ch-2 (second half of Shell), ch 2, 2 LDC in sp **between** 2 sts
**below** next ch-2, skip next 4 LDC, 2 LDC in sp **between**
2 sts **below** next ch-2, ch 2, 2 LDC in sp **between** 2 dc
**below** next ch-2, ch 2, work Shell in next Shell; repeat
from ★ across to last 6 sts, ch 2, 2 LDC in sp **between** 2 sts
**below** next ch-2, ch 2, LDC in sp **between** 2 sts **below** next
ch-2, skip next LDC, dc in last dc.
**Rows 4-6:** Repeat Row 3, 3 times changing to Green in
last dc worked on Row 6 **(Fig. 23a, page 126)**.
**Rows 7-102:** Repeat Row 3, working in the following
Color Sequence: ★ 5 rows Green, 3 rows Beige, 3 rows
Maroon, 5 rows Dk Green; repeat from ★ 5 times **more;**
do **not** finish off at end of Row 102.

## TOP EDGING
**Row 1:** Ch 3, turn; LDC in sp **between** 2 LDC **below**
first ch-2, sc in next 2 dc, 2 LDC in sp **between** 2 dc **below**
next ch-2, sc in next 2 dc, (sc, **ch 2, sc**) in **next** ch-2 sp,
★ (sc in next 2 dc, 2 LDC in sp **between** 2 sts **below** next
ch-2) twice, skip next 4 LDC, (2 LDC in sp **between** 2 sts
**below** next ch-2, sc in next 2 dc) twice, (sc, ch 2, sc) in
next ch-2 sp; repeat from ★ across to last 6 **sts,** sc in next
2 dc, 2 LDC in sp **between** 2 dc **below** next ch-2, sc in
next 2 dc, LDC in sp **between** 2 LDC **below** next ch-2,
dc in last dc.
**Rows 2 and 3:** Ch 1, turn; skip first st, sc in next 8 sts,
(sc, ch 2, sc) in next ch-2 sp, sc in next 8 sts, ★ skip next
2 sts, sc in next 8 sts, (sc, ch 2, sc) in next ch-2 sp, sc in
next 8 sts; repeat from ★ across.
Finish off.

## BOTTOM EDGING
**Row 1:** With **right** side facing and working in free loops of beginning ch *(Fig. 25b, page 126)*, join Dk Green with slip st in first ch; ch 1, sc in same st and in next 8 chs, ★ skip next ch (at base of Shell), sc in next 8 chs, (sc, ch 2, sc) in next ch-2 sp (at point), sc in next 8 chs; repeat from ★ across to last 10 chs, skip next ch, sc in last 9 chs.

**Rows 2 and 3:** Ch 1, turn; 2 sc in first sc, sc in next 7 sc, ★ skip next 2 sc, sc in next 8 sc, (sc, ch 2, sc) in next ch-2 sp, sc in next 8 sc; repeat from ★ across to last 10 sc, skip next 2 sc, sc in next 7 sc, 2 sc in last sc. Finish off.

# GENERAL INSTRUCTIONS

## BASIC INFORMATION

### YARN

Yarn weight (type or size) is divided into four basic categories:
**Fingering** (baby clothes), **Sport** (lightweight sweaters and afghans), **Worsted** (sweaters, afghans, toys), and **Bulky** (heavy sweaters, pot holders, and afghans).
Baby yarn may be classified as either Fingering or Sport — check the label for the recommended gauge.
The weight has absolutely nothing to do with the number of plies. "Ply" refers to the number of strands that have been twisted together to make the yarn. There are fingering weight yarns consisting of four plies, and there are bulky weight yarns made of a single ply.
Yarn listed under Materials for each afghan in this book is given in a generic weight. Once you know the weight of the yarn, any brand of the same weight may be used. This enables you to purchase the brand of yarn you like best. You may wish to purchase a single skein first and crochet a gauge swatch. Compare the way your swatch looks to the photograph to be sure that you will be satisfied with the results. Yardage determines how many skeins to buy. Ounces and grams will vary from one brand of the same weight to another, but the yardage required will always remain the same, provided gauge is met and maintained.

### DYE LOTS

Yarn is dyed in large batches. Each batch is referred to as a "dye lot" and is assigned a number which will be listed on the yarn label. The color will vary slightly in shade from one dye lot to another. This color variance may be noticeable if skeins of yarn from different dye lots are used together in the same project.
Therefore, when purchasing more than one skein of yarn for a particular color in your project, be sure to select skeins of yarn labeled with **identical** dye lot numbers. It is a good practice to purchase an extra skein to be sure that you have enough to complete your project.

### TIPS FOR PURCHASING YARN

1. Always purchase the same weight yarn as specified in your project instructions.
2. It is best to refer to the yardage to determine how many skeins to purchase, since the number of yards per ounce may vary from one brand to another.
3. For each color in your project, purchase skeins in the same dye lot at one time, or you may risk being unable to find the same dye lot again.
4. If you are unsure if you will have enough yarn, buy an extra skein. Some stores will allow you to return unused skeins. Ask your local yarn shop about their return policy.

# HOOKS

Crochet hooks used for working with yarn are made from aluminum, plastic, bone, or wood. They are lettered in sizes ranging from size B (2.25 mm) to the largest, size Q (15.00 mm).

# GAUGE

Gauge is the number of stitches and rows or rounds per inch and is used to determine the finished size of a project. All crochet patterns will specify the gauge that you must match to ensure proper size and to be sure you have enough yarn to complete the project.

Hook size given in instructions is merely a guide. Because everyone crochets differently — loosely, tightly, or somewhere in between — the finished size can vary, even when crocheters use the very same pattern, yarn, and hook.

Before beginning any crocheted item, it is absolutely necessary for you to crochet a gauge swatch in the pattern stitch indicated and with the weight of yarn and hook size suggested. Your swatch must be large enough to measure your gauge. Lay your swatch on a hard, smooth, flat surface. Then measure it, counting your stitches and rows or rounds carefully. If your swatch is smaller than specified or you have too many stitches per inch, try again with a larger size hook; if your swatch is larger or you don't have enough stitches per inch, try again with a smaller size hook. Keep trying until you find the size that will give you the specified gauge. DO NOT HESITATE TO CHANGE HOOK SIZE TO OBTAIN CORRECT GAUGE. Once proper gauge is obtained, measure width of piece approximately every 3" to be sure gauge remains consistent.

# ABBREVIATIONS

| | |
|---|---|
| ch(s) | chain(s) |
| dc | double crochet(s) |
| dtr | double treble crochet(s) |
| FPhdc | Front Post half double crochet(s) |
| FPtr | Front Post treble crochet(s) |
| hdc | half double crochet(s) |
| mm | millimeters |
| Rnd(s) | Round(s) |
| sc | single crochet(s) |
| sp(s) | space(s) |
| st(s) | stitch(es) |
| tr | treble crochet(s) |
| Tr tr | triple treble crochet(s) |
| YO | yarn over |

★ — work instructions following ★ as many **more** times as indicated in addition to the first time.

† to † or ♥ to ♥ — work all instructions from first † to second † or from first ♥ to second ♥ **as many** times as specified.

( ) or [ ] — work enclosed instructions **as many** times as specified by the number immediately following **or** work all enclosed instructions in the stitch or space indicated **or** contains explanatory remarks.

# TERMS

**chain loosely** — work the chain **only** loose enough for the hook to pass through the chain easily when working the next row or round into the chain.

**multiple** — the number of stitches required to complete one repeat of a pattern.

**post** — the vertical shaft of a stitch.

**right side vs. wrong side** — the **right** side of your work is the side that will show when the piece is finished.

**work across or around** — continue working in the established pattern.

# BASIC STITCH GUIDE

## CHAIN

To work a chain stitch, begin with a slip knot on the hook. Bring the yarn **over** hook from **back** to **front**, catching the yarn with the hook and turning the hook slightly toward you to keep the yarn from slipping off. Draw the yarn through the slip knot **(Fig. 1)** (chain made, *abbreviated ch*).

Fig. 1

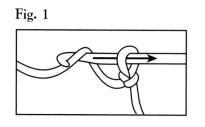

## WORKING INTO THE CHAIN

When beginning a row of crochet in a chain, always skip the first chain from the hook, and work into the second chain from hook (for single crochet) or third chain from hook (for half double crochet), etc. **(Fig. 2a)**.

Fig. 2a

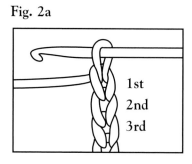

Method 1: Insert hook under top two strands of each chain **(Fig. 2b)**.
Method 2: Insert hook into back ridge of each chain **(Fig. 2c)**.

Fig. 2b

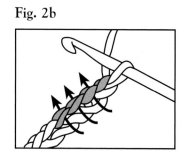

Fig. 2c

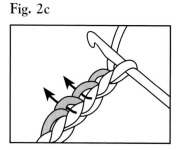

## SLIP STITCH

This stitch is used to attach new yarn, to join work, or to move the yarn across a group of stitches without adding height. Insert hook in stitch or space indicated, YO and draw through stitch **and** loop on hook **(Fig. 3)** (slip stitch made, *abbreviated slip st*).

Fig. 3

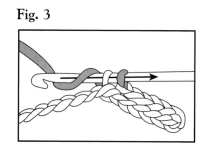

## SINGLE CROCHET

Insert hook in stitch or space indicated, YO and pull up a loop (2 loops on hook), YO and draw through both loops on hook **(Fig. 4)** (single crochet made, *abbreviated sc*).

Fig. 4

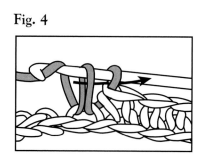

## HALF DOUBLE CROCHET

YO, insert hook in stitch or space indicated, YO and pull up a loop (3 loops on hook), YO and draw through all 3 loops on hook **(Fig. 5)** (half double crochet made, *abbreviated hdc*).

Fig. 5

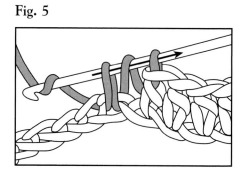

# DOUBLE CROCHET

YO, insert hook in stitch or space indicated, YO and pull up a loop (3 loops on hook), YO and draw through 2 loops on hook **(Fig. 6a)**, YO and draw through remaining 2 loops on hook **(Fig. 6b)** (double crochet made, *abbreviated dc*).

**Fig. 6a**

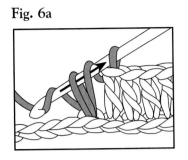

**Fig. 6b**

# TREBLE CROCHET

YO twice, insert hook in stitch or space indicated, YO and pull up a loop (4 loops on hook) **(Fig. 7a)**, (YO and draw through 2 loops on hook) 3 times **(Fig. 7b)** (treble crochet made, *abbreviated tr*).

**Fig. 7a**

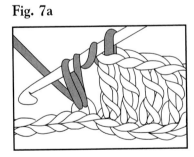

**Fig. 7b**

# DOUBLE TREBLE CROCHET

YO 3 times, insert hook in stitch or space indicated, YO and pull up a loop (5 loops on hook) **(Fig. 8a)**, (YO and draw through 2 loops on hook) 4 times **(Fig. 8b)** (double treble crochet made, *abbreviated dtr*).

**Fig. 8a**

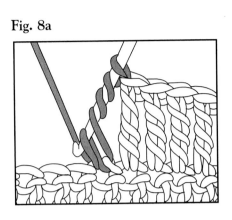

**Fig. 8b**

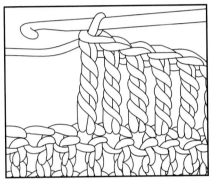

# TRIPLE TREBLE CROCHET

YO 4 times, insert hook in stitch or space indicated, YO and pull up a loop (6 loops on hook) **(Fig. 9a)**, (YO and draw through 2 loops on hook) 5 times **(Fig. 9b)** (triple treble crochet made, *abbreviated Tr tr*).

**Fig. 9a**     **Fig. 9b**

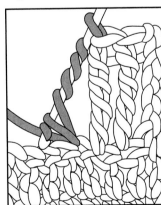 

# PATTERN STITCHES

## POST STITCH

Work around post of stitch indicated, inserting hook in direction of arrow (*Fig. 10*).

### Fig. 10

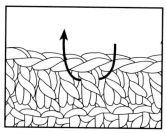

## FRONT POST HALF DOUBLE CROCHET

YO, insert hook from **front** to **back** around post of stitch indicated (*Fig. 10*), YO and pull up a loop (3 loops on hook) (*Fig. 11*), YO and draw through all 3 loops on hook (**Front Post half double crochet made,** *abbreviated FPhdc*).

### Fig. 11

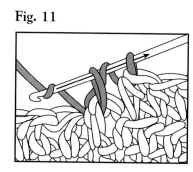

## FRONT POST TREBLE CROCHET

YO twice, insert hook from **front** to **back** around post of stitch indicated (*Fig. 10*), YO and pull up a loop (4 loops on hook) (*Fig. 12*), (YO and draw through 2 loops on hook) 3 times (**Front Post treble crochet made,** *abbreviated FPtr*).

### Fig. 12

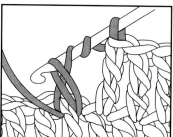

## HDC IN POST OF STITCH

YO, insert hook in post of dc just made in direction of arrow (*Fig. 13*), YO and pull up a loop, YO and draw through all 3 loops on hook.

### Fig. 13

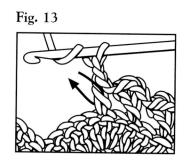

## POPCORN

Work 4 or 5 sts in stitch or space indicated, drop loop from hook, insert hook in first st of group, hook dropped loop and draw through (*Fig. 14*).

### Fig. 14

## PUFF STITCH

★ YO, insert hook in st or sp indicated, YO and pull up a loop even with loop on hook; repeat from ★ as many times as specified, YO and draw through all loops on hook (*Fig. 15*).

### Fig. 15

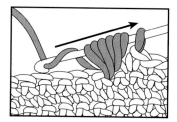

# CLUSTER

A Cluster can be worked all in the same stitch or space (**Figs. 16a & b**), **or** across several stitches (**Figs. 16c & d**).

### Fig. 16a

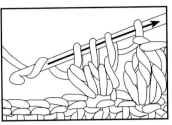

### Fig. 16b

### Fig. 16c

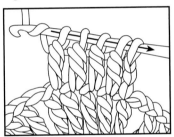

### Fig. 16d

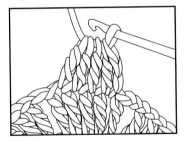

# LONG STITCH

Work single crochet (**sc**), double crochet (**dc**), or treble crochet (**tr**), inserting hook in stitch indicated in instructions and pulling up a loop even with loop on hook; complete stitch (**Fig. 17**).

### Fig. 17

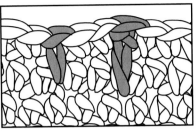

# LONG SINGLE CROCHET

Insert hook from front to back **around** center ring of Pansy between second and third 3-dc groups, YO and pull up a loop, YO and draw through both loops on hook (**Fig. 18**) (**long single crochet made,** *abbreviated LSC*).

### Fig. 18

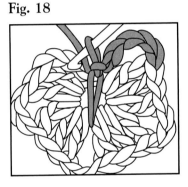

# REVERSE SINGLE CROCHET

Working from **left** to **right**, ★ insert hook in st to right of hook **(Fig. 19a)**, YO and draw through, under, and to left of loop on hook (2 loops on hook) **(Fig. 19b)**, YO and draw through both loops on hook **(Fig. 19c)** **(reverse sc made, Fig. 19d)**; repeat from ★.

**Fig. 19a**

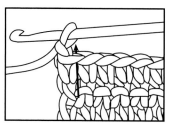

**Fig. 19b**

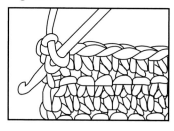

**Fig. 19c**

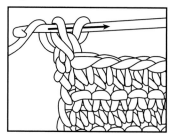

**Fig. 19d**

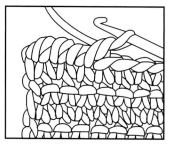

# WORKING BETWEEN STITCHES

When insructed to work in space **before** a stitch or in spaces **between** stitches, insert hook in space indicated by arrow **(Fig. 20)**.

**Fig. 20**

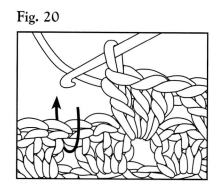

# NO-SEW JOINING

Hold pieces with **wrong** sides together. Slip stitch or sc into stitch or space indicated **(Fig. 21)**.

**Fig. 21**

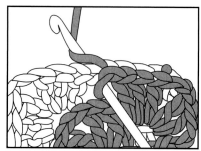

# CROSS STITCH

Add cross stitch design to each Block *(Fig. 22)*, following Charts below. Each square on the Charts represents one cross stitch. Each cross stitch is worked over a center ch-1 sp into ch-1 sps around center ch-1 sp. To center design, use marked ch-1 on Block matched to center stitch on Chart. Using yarn needle and long strand of yarn doubled, weave end under several stitches on back of piece to secure (do not tie knot). With **right** side facing and Row 51 of Block at top, work cross stitches as follows: bring needle up at 1, down at 2 (half cross made), up at 3, down at 4 **(cross stitch completed, *Fig. 22*)**. All cross stitches should cross in the same direction. Finish off by weaving end under several stitches on back; cut close to work.

Following Charts, add designs to Blocks as follows: 3 Bears, 3 Deer, 4 Moose, and 10 Trees.

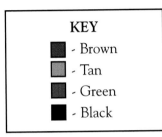

KEY
- ■ - Brown
- ▨ - Tan
- ▦ - Green
- ■ - Black

 Fig. 22

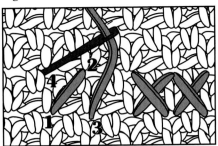

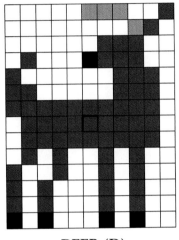

**DEER (D)**

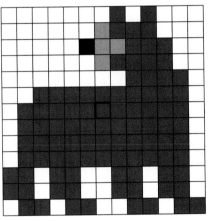

**BEAR (B)**

**MOOSE (M)**

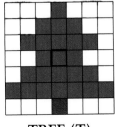

**TREE (T)**

# STITCHING TIPS

## CHANGING COLORS

Work the last stitch to within one step of completion, hook new yarn **(Fig. 23a)** and draw through all loops on hook. Cut old yarn and work over both ends.
When working in rounds, drop old yarn and join with slip stitch to first stitch using new yarn **(Fig. 23b)**.

**Fig. 23a**

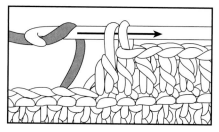

**Fig. 23b**

## BACK OR FRONT LOOP ONLY

Work only in loop(s) indicated by arrow **(Fig. 24)**.

**Fig. 24**

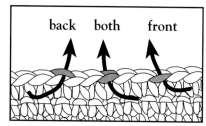

## FREE LOOPS

After working in Back or Front Loops Only on a row or round, there will be a ridge of unused loops. These are called the free loops. Later, when instructed to work in the free loops of same row or round, work in these loops **(Fig. 25a)**. When instructed to work in free loops of a beginning ch, work in loop indicated by arrow **(Fig. 25b)**.

**Fig. 25a**

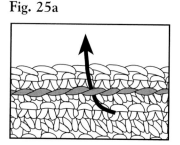

**Fig. 25b**

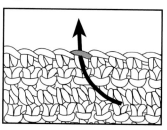

## JOINING WITH SC

When instructed to join with sc, begin with a slip knot on hook. Insert hook in stitch or space indicated, YO and pull up a loop, YO and draw through both loops on hook.

# FINISHING

## WHIPSTITCH

With **wrong** sides together and beginning in stitch indicated, sew through both pieces once to secure the beginning of the seam, leaving an ample yarn end to weave in later. Insert the needle from **right** to **left** through **inside** loops of each piece **(Fig. 26a) or** through **both** loops **(Fig. 26b)**. Bring the needle around and insert it from **right** to **left** through the next loops of **both** pieces. Repeat along the edge, keeping the sewing yarn fairly loose and being careful to match stitches.

**Fig. 26a**

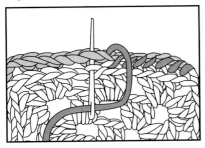

**Fig. 26b**

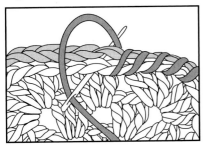

## TASSEL

Cut a piece of cardboard 3" wide and as long as you want your finished tassel to be. Wind a double strand of yarn around the cardboard approximately 12 times. Cut an 18" length of yarn and insert it under all of the strands at the top of the cardboard; pull up **tightly** and tie securely. Leave the yarn ends long enough to attach the tassel. Cut the yarn at the opposite end of the cardboard and then remove it **(Fig. 27a)**. Cut a 6" length of yarn and wrap it **tightly** around the tassel twice, 1" below the top **(Fig. 27b)**; tie securely. Trim the ends.

**Fig. 27a**          **Fig. 27b**

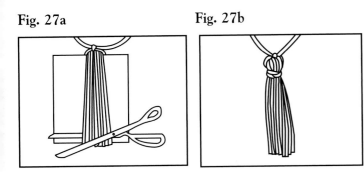

## FRINGE

Cut a piece of cardboard 3" wide and 1/2" longer than desired fringe. Wind the yarn **loosely** and **evenly** around the cardboard until the card is filled, then cut across one end; repeat as needed.

Align the number of strands desired and fold in half. With **wrong** side facing and using a crochet hook, draw the folded end up through a stitch or row and pull the loose ends through the folded end **(Figs. 28a & c)**; draw the knot up **tightly (Figs. 28b & d)**. Repeat, spacing as desired.

Lay flat on a hard surface and trim the ends.

**Fig. 28a**          **Fig. 28b**

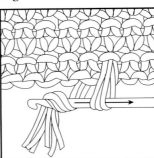

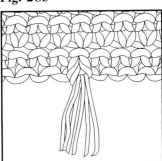

**Fig. 28c**          **Fig. 28d**

# CREDITS

To Magna IV Color Imaging of Little Rock, Arkansas, we say thank you for the superb color reproduction and excellent pre-press preparation.

We want to especially thank photographers Ken West, Larry Pennington, Mark Mathews, and Karen Shirey of Peerless Photography, Little Rock, Arkansas, and Jerry R. Davis of Jerry Davis Photography, Little Rock, Arkansas, for their time, patience, and excellent work.

We would like to extend a special word of thanks to the talented designers who created the lovely projects in this book:

Eleanor Albano: *Cozy Clusters*, page 62, and *American Fireworks*, page 112

Alexander-Stratton: *Country Garden*, page 12, and *Baby-Soft Wrap*, page 96

Judy Bolin: *Honeycomb Flower Patch*, page 82

Polly Carbonari: *Woodland Warmer*, page 70

Nair Carswell: *Sunflower Festival*, page 10

Juanita Lanham Froese: *Chain of Hearts*, page 36

Sarah J. Green: *Sweetheart Plaid*, page 106

Anne Halliday: *Rosy Lullaby*, page 22; *Ring Around the Roses*, page 26; *Delightful Daffodils*, page 28; *In Love with Lace*, page 34; *Peek-a-Boo Hearts*, page 38; *Country at Heart*, page 44; *Summer Lace*, page 76; *Rambling Rose*, page 100; and *Shamrock Ripple*, page 108

Jan Hatfield: *Crisscross Cover-up*, page 54; *Hearthside Ridges*, page 56; and *Timeless Tracks*, page 58

Terry Kimbrough: *Pansy Romance*, page 14, and *Wildflower Bouquets*, page 18

Anne Kirtley: *Queen's Trellis*, page 92

Jennine Korejko: *Primrose Path*, page 16

Cynthia Lark: *Floral Daydream*, page 6

Melissa Leapman: *Glowing Embers*, page 52, and *Wintry Fans*, page 102

Roberta Maier: *Blue & White China*, page 74

Sarah Anne Phillips: *Pretty Posies*, page 8

Carole Prior: *Dogwood Blossoms*, page 20; *Spring Garden*, page 24; *Sweetheart Baby Wrap*, page 42; *Relaxing Ripple*, page 60; *Teal Tapestry*, page 66; *Striking Stripes*, page 68; *Granny's Rose Garden*, page 78; *Parlor Fans*, page 80; *Old-fashioned Roses*, page 84; *Lickety-Split Log Cabin*, page 86; *Nostalgic Ripple*, page 94; and *Easter Granny*, page 110

Katherine Satterfield Robert: *Baby's Pretty Pillowghan*, page 46

Rhonda Semonis: *Airy Heirloom*, page 90

Martha Brooks Stein: *Patchwork Hearts*, page 40; *Patchwork Quilts*, page 64; *Patchwork Memories*, page 88; and *Nine-Patch Spools*, page 98